In this little book, Paul  far-flung journey thro about anxiety. He does heavily emphasizes practical ways we can reflect on, and in many cases act on, the insights Tautges unearths in the passages he chooses. His relentless call to us to thoughtfully connect the many hopes we have in Christ with our daily experiences of fear and anxiety would be impossible for us to engage without the significant benefit to our faith and comfort that we find in Christ.

—**Alasdair Groves**, Executive Director, Christian Counseling and Educational Foundation (CCEF) New England; Director, CCEF School of Biblical Counseling

This devotional came at just the right time in my own life, as everyday worries and anxieties had nudged my gaze away from Jesus Christ. I'm thankful for this new resource from the pen of a fellow struggler who bravely and honestly wrestles with the perennial problem of anxiety. Read it each day and be comforted, convicted, and ultimately conformed into the image of Christ, who takes all our cares and burdens onto himself.

—**Jonathan Holmes**, Pastor of Counseling, Parkside Church, Chagrin Falls, Ohio; Founder and Executive Director, Fieldstone Counseling

Tautges, with vulnerable transparency, offers wise counsel in this small yet critical work on anxiety. He allows Scripture to define this raw and often paralyzing emotion as he finds deep and lasting hope in the powerful truths of God's Word. His gentle explanations and careful admonitions act as a guard and guide to all who wrestle with perpetual fear and anxious thoughts.

—**T. Dale Johnson**, Executive Director, Association of Certified Biblical Counselors; Associate Professor of Biblical Counseling, Midwestern Baptist Theological Seminary

I love the way Paul Tautges grabs anxiety by the horns, wrestles it to the ground, and defeats its insidious deception through clear, wise biblical counsel. He helps the reader to understand what anxiety is, how destructive it is, and how to successfully defeat it. Most of all, I'm impressed with the way that my friend offers concise, practical steps that empower the reader to overcome fear and anxiety. There is so much I love about this little book, and I give it a hearty double-thumbs-up!

—**Joni Eareckson Tada**, Founder/CEO, Joni and Friends International Disability Center

One in five people suffer from chronic anxiety. Even more people experience episodes of anxiety. This month-long daily devotional offers biblical wisdom for this common problem. Paul Tautges, a respected pastor and counselor, has the experience and gospel focus to help the anxiety sufferer. He describes the nature of anxiety and brings the power of the gospel and the comforts of the Savior to bear on this problem. This is practical, accessible help for sufferers of anxiety.

—**Tedd Tripp**, Pastor; Author; Conference Speaker

ANXIETY

TRUTH FOR LIFE®

THE BIBLE-TEACHING MINISTRY OF **ALISTAIR BEGG**

The mission of Truth For Life is to teach the Bible with clarity and relevance so that unbelievers will be converted, believers will be established, and local churches will be strengthened.

Daily Program
Each day, Truth For Life distributes the Bible teaching of Alistair Begg across the U.S. and in several locations outside of the U.S. through 1,700 radio outlets. To find a radio station near you, visit **truthforlife.org/stationfinder**.

Free Teaching
The daily program, and Truth For Life's entire teaching archive of over 2,000 Bible-teaching messages, can be accessed for free online and through Truth For Life's full-feature mobile app. Download the free mobile app at **truthforlife.org/app** and listen free online at **truthforlife.org**.

At-Cost Resources
Books and full-length teaching from Alistair Begg on CD, DVD, and USB are available for purchase at cost, with no markup. Visit **truthforlife.org/store**.

Where to Begin?
If you're new to Truth For Life and would like to know where to begin listening and learning, find starting point suggestions at **truthforlife.org/firststep**. For a full list of ways to connect with Truth For Life, visit **truthforlife.org/subscribe**.

Contact Truth For Life
P.O. Box 398000 Cleveland, Ohio 44139
phone 1 (888) 588-7884 **email** letters@truthforlife.org
 /truthforlife @truthforlife truthforlife.org

ANXIETY

KNOWING
GOD'S PEACE

PAUL TAUTGES

PUBLISHING
P.O. BOX 817 • PHILLIPSBURG • NEW JERSEY 08865-0817

Library of Congress Cataloging-in-Publication Data

Names: Tautges, Paul, author.
Title: Anxiety : knowing God's peace / Paul Tautges.
Description: Phillipsburg, NJ : P&R Publishing, [2019] | Series: 31-day devotionals for life's problems | Includes bibliographical references.
Identifiers: LCCN 2019013788| ISBN 9781629956220 (pbk.) | ISBN 9781629956237 (epub) | ISBN 9781629956244 (mobi)
Subjects: LCSH: Anxiety--Religious aspects--Christianity--Meditations. | Peace of mind--Religious aspects--Christianity--Meditations.
Classification: LCC BV4908.5 .T38 2019 | DDC 242/.4--dc23
LC record available at https://lccn.loc.gov/2019013788

Contents

Tips for Reading This Devotional

EARLY IN OUR marriage, my wife and I lived on the top floor of a town house, in a small one-bedroom apartment. Whenever it rained, leaks in the roof would drip through the ceiling and onto our floors. I remember placing buckets in different parts of the apartment and watching the water slowly drip, one drop at a time. I put large buckets out and thought, *It'll take a while to fill them.* The water built up over time, and often I was surprised at how quickly those buckets filled up, overflowing if I didn't pay close enough attention.

This devotional is just like rain filling up a bucket. It's slow, and it builds over time. Just a few verses every day. Drip. Drip. Drip. Just a few drops of Scripture daily to satiate your parched soul.

We start with Scripture. God's Word is powerful. In fact, it's the most powerful force in the entire universe.[1] It turns the hearts of kings, brings comfort to the lowly, and gives spiritual sight to the blind. It transforms lives and turns them upside down. We know that the Bible is God's very own words, so we read and study it to know God himself.

Our study of Scripture is practical. Theology should change how we live. It's crucial to connect the Word with your struggles. Often, as you read this devotional, you'll see the word *you* because Paul speaks directly to you, the reader. The readings contain a mixture of reflection questions and practical suggestions. You'll get much more from this experience if you answer the questions and do the practical exercises. Don't skip them. Do them for the sake of your own soul.

Our study of Scripture is worshipful. Anxiety can ruin your life. And, fundamentally, any struggle with anxiety is a worship problem. You might be preoccupied with financial struggles, sickness, troubles at work, a rebellious teenager, or some other problem. These things are the objects of your anxiety, and they consume a lot of your time and energy. Yet your anxiety is *first* a problem with God. Is the Lord really sovereign over your life? Does the peace of Christ reign in your heart? "We're not going to have enough to pay the bills." "I'll be in pain for months." "My boss hates me." "My son just doesn't care anymore." There is a war in your heart, and your anxiety is a manifestation of that war. There is no inner peace, only turmoil, on many days. As pressures come from outside you, and worries bubble up within you, you realize that you can't do battle on your own.

You've probably picked up this devotional because your anxiety is hurting your life. Let me commend you; that's an important step. But let me also point out that defeating anxiety is not a matter of getting rid of our troubles (as helpful as it might be to get rid of some of them) or of finding healthy ways to manage our out-of-control emotions (though that's useful too) but of first turning back to the Lord for his help. The Word points us to Christ, who rescues us from our anxiety and reorients our life. We can find rest. An inner peace comes through Christ.

"Take heart." "Have courage." "Do not be afraid." These are common phrases in Scripture. There are no quick fixes when it comes to defeating anxiety. Fighting it will require orienting your entire life to Christ. Your goal in fighting your anxiety should always be worship of him.

If you find this devotional helpful (and I trust that you will!), reread it in different seasons of your life. Work through it this coming month, and then come back to it a year from now, to remind yourself how to do battle with your anxiety.

This devotional is *not* meant to be a comprehensive guide to fighting anxiety. Good volumes are already written for that purpose. Buy them and make good use of them. You'll see several resources listed at the end of the book.

That's enough for now. Let's begin.

Deepak Reju

INTRODUCTION

When Panic Attacks

SIX YEARS AGO, I could not have written this book. I was a prisoner. Anxiety crippled me and held me captive. Satan took advantage of an extended season of depression I was going through that had been triggered by the impact of a myriad of difficulties in our church and family. Mounting pressure from every direction, along with my own angry response to it, collided to create a swirling storm of fear. I had experienced anxiety before, but never like this. I couldn't go on. Some days, I didn't even want to.

Twice I went to the emergency room showing symptoms of a heart attack. After my second trip to the ER, my physician sent me to a cardiologist to get blood work and a stress test. The tests determined that I hadn't had an actual heart attack (the kind that causes permanent damage to the heart muscle) but a stress-induced heart problem that causes only short-term harm.

The Mayo Clinic calls it *broken heart syndrome*[1]—a temporary heart condition that is brought on by stressful situations or grievous loss. It involves a surge of stress hormones disrupting the heart's normal pumping function. This condition mimics a heart attack by causing a similar set of symptoms, including chest pain, shortness of breath, an irregular heartbeat, and generalized weakness. When this occurs, people believe they are having a heart attack. I did—twice, in less than a year. And what I experienced is more common than I knew.

Perhaps you can relate to one or more parts of my story. Perhaps not. Regardless, we all struggle with various forms of anxiety.

What does *your* anxiety look like? Is it mild worry? Or full-blown panic? Or something in between? Did you pick up this devotional because feelings of anxiousness come and go—or because they are constant? No matter what your anxiety looks like, the Bible speaks truth and peace into your mind and heart. Scripture directly addresses the anxious heart in helpful ways.

Anxiety Is Entwined with Our Bodies

Anxiety is a persistent part of our human condition. It's so common that an estimated 23 million Americans suffer from panic attacks, while millions more identify themselves as having some form of anxiety disorder. It is helpful to realize how honestly the Scriptures uncover this side of human experience, shed light on the effect that anxiety has on our bodies (and vice versa), and fuel the faith that strengthens inner security and peace.

Thousands of years ago, Jewish patriarchs recognized the impact of powerful emotions on the body. For example, Jacob feared the possibility of premature death from deep sorrow and distress (see Gen. 37:35; 42:38; 44:29). When his son Judah pleaded for Joseph to release his youngest brother Benjamin, he specifically begged to be allowed to return Benjamin to his father. Judah said, "As soon as I come to your servant my father, and the boy is not with us, then, as his life is bound up in the boy's life, as soon as he sees that the boy is not with us, he will die, and your servants will bring down the gray hairs of your servant our father with sorrow to Sheol"—that is, to the grave by premature death (Gen. 44:30–31).

The Bible also contains examples of the reverse happening—of anxiety being caused by physical suffering. The author of Psalm 102 pleaded with God to listen to him in his distress, which was not connected to his sin but occurred alongside his physical afflictions (see vv. 3–5). Job, too, is an example of this. As the result of immense loss and excruciating bodily pain, he experienced deep anxiety. "I have no peace, no quietness; I have no rest, but only turmoil" (Job 3:26 NIV). Even the apostle Paul experienced burdens that were "beyond [his] strength" (2 Cor. 1:8). It does not take much imagination to see how his mental suffering was a consequence of physical suffering.[2]

Scripture Heals Our Souls

Not only is our physical frame custom-made by God, but so is our emotional makeup (see Ps. 139:13–14)![3] We are so amazingly designed by God that he should be exalted and praised—though the full interplay of our bodies and spirits, as well as the understanding of our beautiful and yet complicated emotions, remain mysterious to us.

One thing is clear, however: *we are always made up of body and soul . . . together . . . always.* Regardless of what physical elements may contribute to our anxiety, every mental or emotional struggle we experience is also an opportunity to develop our faith. Our souls are *always* in need of the Spirit's ministry of grace and truth through the Word.

I'm not a physician, but I am a "soul doctor"—a pastor who wants to help you connect with the healing words of Scripture so that mental and emotional peace will reign in your heart, despite whatever physical or circumstantial challenges you face.

The Goal of This Book

When panic attacks, it truly does feel as if an enemy is attacking us. Debilitating fear strikes us out of nowhere. We don't always know why we're anxious. Though external pressures do act as triggers, and while some anxiety arises from physical problems, fundamentally there is something going on in our inner person. Fears and doubts hijack our peace, inner turmoil ensues, and our hearts pound.

"Anxiety in a man's heart weighs him down, but a good word makes him glad" (Prov. 12:25). This proverb hardly needs explanation. Anxiety in our hearts troubles our spirits, which in turn affects our bodies. Although anxiety sometimes arises from malfunctions in our bodies, this devotional addresses anxiety that is connected to the soul. Anxiety weakens us—it drags us down. But there is something that lifts us up and makes us glad: a good word—whether from God in Scripture or from a faithful friend.

In this book, I aim to bring you both. I want to bring you healing words by coming alongside you as an encouraging friend. I hope to enter your personal struggle with anxiety by allowing you to enter mine—to open a window to my heart in order to share biblical truths that the Lord continues to use in order to help bring me greater peace.

Peace is a recurring theme in this devotional; you will see it crop up again and again. I will help you to understand not only what a peaceful state of mind looks like but also how to maintain that state of mind by training the eyes of your heart to habitually look to the Lord. Additionally, I will help you to understand the connection between the peace *of* God and peace *with* God. In other words, the experience of the peace *of* God flows out of an ever-deepening awareness of being securely at peace *with* God through faith in his Son.

How We Will Get There

To reach the goal of knowing God's peace—not only in our heads but in our hearts—we will take a 31-day walk together. First we will *define* anxiety. I will do this by opening up Scripture's abundant pantry of truth in order to feed our souls. I will also shine a flashlight on the real-life experiences of men and women in the Bible who, like us, struggled with anxiety. Once this foundation of understanding is laid, we will look at the character of God and see how his promises speak to our anxiety. In the final and longest section, I will open a chest of biblical wisdom to show you practical ways you can *fight* anxiety.

It's really important for you to patiently press through the first part of this devotional. Just as, when you are building a house, the strength of the concrete foundation will determine the durability of the wooden structure, the better you understand what anxiety is (in part 1), the more successful you will be at knowing God's peace experientially as you apply his resources (in part 2) to the fight (in part 3).

So let's start walking. Together, let's ask God to renew our minds and to help us learn to trust him with our anxiety.

A Brief Word on Medication

IF YOU ARE experiencing the symptoms of a panic attack or broken heart syndrome, you should see your doctor right away for a thorough medical checkup in order to discover, or exclude, any physical problems that may be causing your symptoms of anxiety. The relationship between the body and soul is complex, and respecting medical counsel is wise. For some people, using a symptom-relieving medication for a limited time may help them to get control of their escalated emotional state. Others may find that the benefits of medication do not offset its side effects—or even that it has significant downsides.[1]

For example, at one point, my physician believed that a short-term use of anxiety medication might help to pull me through a crisis and prevent further damage. However, instead of calming down my anxiety so that my body could begin to repair itself, the medication increased it dramatically—producing a sense of terror, impending doom, and even a desire for death. We set the medication aside and agreed that major, life-altering decisions were necessary instead. In contrast, Bob, another counselor and minister of the gospel, was meaningfully helped by medicine. In his story, he says, "The medicine helped stabilize me so that I could think rationally and apply biblical principles to my situation."[2]

Mental fog often accompanies severe anxiety. Therefore, any decision that you make concerning the use or non-use of medication must be well-informed, humbly bathed in prayer and clothed in counsel, and under the guidance and supervision of your personal physician.

DEFINING ANXIETY

DAY 1

Anxiety Distracts Us

"Therefore I tell you, do not be anxious about your life, what you will eat or what you will drink, nor about your body, what you will put on. Is not life more than food, and the body more than clothing?" (Matt. 6:25)

ANXIETY IS SO much a part of our lives that it's natural for us to talk about it frequently. However, *defining* it, and understanding how it works, sometimes seems like trying to nail Jell-O to the wall. Anxiety is an emotion—but it's more than a feeling. It often includes a physical reaction—but it's more than that, too. So what *is* anxiety, exactly?

The writers of the New Testament employ two different, but related, words to refer to the experience that we call anxiety. They combine the noun *merimna*, which is usually translated "care," with the verb *merizo*, which means to draw in different directions or distract. To be anxious, then, means to have a *distracting care*—to have our minds and hearts torn between two worlds. We see this in Jesus's warning about thorns choking out the Word of God, which is intended to produce faith. He identifies these thorns as "the cares of the world" (Mark 4:19) or "the cares and riches and pleasures of life" (Luke 8:14). Anxious cares are typically tied to our earthly lives and are most often temporal, not eternal.

These distracting cares divide our mental energy and cloud our spiritual vision; they keep us focused on the here-and-now instead of on the future-promised-but-not-yet. They form cataracts over our spiritual eyes and hinder us from keeping heavenly things in clear focus or from keeping diligent watch for the Lord's return (see Luke 21:34).

Anxiety diverts us from what is most important. It causes our eyes to see only what is before us at that very moment. Our worries exert great effort to keep our vision fixed on the *horizontal* (the things of the world) instead of on the *vertical* (the things of God).

In today's passage, Jesus commands us not to be anxious about our food or drink or clothing. He then immediately directs us to "look" somewhere else (Matt. 6:26). By looking at the birds of the air and the flowers of the field, we shift our focus to the heavenly Father who promises to provide even better care for us than he does for them.

Instead of allowing our minds to be distracted by the troubles of today, Jesus tells us to "seek first the kingdom of God and his righteousness, and all these things will be added to you" (Matt. 6:33). As we renew our minds and discipline our hearts to keep eternal matters as our central priority, we learn to rest in God, who has promised to meet all our needs. Therefore, even when our personal responsibilities require a certain amount of our attention, we can always look to the Lord with confidence rather than being fearful.

Reflect: What earthly cares are currently distracting you? What preoccupies your mind?

Reflect: Anxiety distracts you with temporal matters, but Jesus reminds you to keep eternal matters central.

Act: In a journal or notebook, write down everything you are currently anxious about. Then turn this "care list" into a "prayer list"—take each care to the Lord and ask him to show you which of them relate to your responsibilities, which you need to act on, and which you need to entrust (release) to him in faith.

DAY 2

Anxiety Weighs Us Down

*And, apart from other things, there is the daily pressure on
me of my anxiety for all the churches. (2 Cor. 11:28)*

YESTERDAY WE SAW that anxiety can be defined as "distracting care." Today Paul introduces us to another way of viewing it. In 2 Corinthians 11:28, the apostle describes his anxiety as *pressure*—as the burden of the physical or mental distress he feels "for all the churches" he has helped to start or shepherd. We can only imagine how many people and needs this would have entailed. And if that weren't enough, this "daily pressure" comes *on top of* "other things" he has already mentioned—including "imprisonments" and "countless beatings," being shipwrecked and surrounded by all kinds of dangers, and personal hardships such as sleeplessness, hunger, and thirst (see 2 Cor. 11:23–27). Pressure on top of pressure. Talk about anxiety!

Paul's pressures were sometimes accompanied by despair (see 2 Cor. 1:8). This shouldn't surprise us, since many people experience depression alongside anxiety. But Paul always knew where to turn—to "the God of all comfort"—and so he assures us that God "comforts us in all our affliction" (2 Cor. 1:3–4). This truth is for *all* believers throughout *all* time.

Paul wrote this comforting promise while in the furnace of personal affliction. His mental suffering was so extreme that he and his companions were "utterly burdened beyond [their] strength" and "despaired of life itself" (2 Cor. 1:8). Nevertheless, these servants of God turned the eyes of their hearts to Christ.

Perhaps you are thinking, "I'm not an apostle. How does this help me?" Let me show you two ways that it does.

First, Paul reminds us that God graciously orchestrates

suffering to strip his children of self-reliance—of the pride that feeds so many of our other sins and hinders our usefulness. In the case of the apostle and his friends, God used overwhelming pressures to accomplish their Christian growth and perseverance. "That was to make us rely not on ourselves but on God who raises the dead," they said (2 Cor. 1:9). Setting our hope on God alone, not on the lessening of our pressure or on the improvement of our circumstances, is the ultimate remedy for anxiety.

Second, the example of Paul and his friends directs us to discipline ourselves to look to Jesus. Their testimony was that "on him we have set our hope" (2 Cor. 1:10). Hope delivers us from the crippling effects of anxiety, because it helps us to cling to an immovable anchor: the truth that God is for us in Jesus Christ (see Rom. 8:31). The promise of ultimate deliverance in Jesus breathed life into the suffering apostles so that they could press on in the midst of unbearable pressure. The same is true for you and me. When we have moments of panic, we can stop, take control of our thought processes, and choose to believe that God's love for us in Christ is greater than any pressure that tries to hijack our peace.

Reflect: What might the God of providence be seeking to accomplish in your heart through your current trials?

Act: Memorize Romans 8:31. As you review this verse, meditate on God's love for you and on the eternal security you possess in Christ.

Act: What are some of the "other things" in your life that contribute to the pressure you are feeling? Talk to the Lord about these things.

DAY 3

We Are Embodied Spirits

Be gracious to me, O Lord, for I am in distress; my eye is wasted from grief; my soul and my body also. . . . My strength fails because of my iniquity, and my bones waste away. Because of all my adversaries I have become a reproach. . . . I have been forgotten like one who is dead; I have become like a broken vessel. (Ps. 31:9–12)

PSALM 31 ILLUSTRATES the interplay of our bodies and souls in our suffering and acknowledges that our frailties make us susceptible to emotional struggles like anxiety. Look at the layers of trouble that were all heaped on King David at the same time, which resulted in his having a heightened level of anxiety:

- physical weakness ("my strength fails . . . my bones waste away")
- a conscience that was troubled by sin ("because of my iniquity")
- hostility from his opponents ("because of all my adversaries")
- abusive treatment from others ("I have become a reproach")
- betrayal by his friends ("I have been forgotten like one who is dead")

No wonder his soul and body—his whole person—were in "distress"!

The word *distress* implies mental strain or stress that is caused by danger or trouble and is impacting the body. It's a vivid picture of the powerful effects of anxiety on a person's inner and outer strength. It's also a reminder of the way that challenging circumstances outside the body can aggravate anguish in the soul.

Because of his distress, David needs help and assurance from God that his whole person—both his body and soul—are in God's caring hands. And so he prays.

"Be gracious to me, O Lord" is his simple yet bold cry. Though he is helpless, David's desperate prayer reveals that he still has hope that God will eventually come to his aid. Clearly his faith is feeble in the moment; he finds it difficult to rest in God— to trust him as he slowly crawls through his personal fog. And yet he still calls out to God. He consciously moves from anxiety to assurance by personalizing the Bible's truth—by choosing to hide by faith in God, who is his "rock of refuge" and "strong fortress" (Ps. 31:2). Later in the same psalm, David reiterates his dependence on the Lord—which, while unavoidable, he also makes a choice to submit to: "But I trust in you, O Lord; I say, 'You are my God. My times are in your hand'" (vv. 14–15).

In what ways might anxiety be affecting your body or sense of strength? Are you reaching out to God for the empowering grace that you need today? Do you see yourself moving from anxiety to assurance?

Ultimately, security and peace come from the Lord—from knowing and trusting the character and love of God. So don't let your anxiety lead you away from God. Run to him today.

Reflect: When you are anxious, do you cry out to God or fight your anxiety alone? Why?

Reflect: Durable faith reaches for joy, even in the midst of distress: "I will rejoice and be glad in your steadfast love, because you have seen my affliction" (Ps. 31:7). How can you choose the path of joy?

Act: In a notebook or journal, write out a prayer that admits your needs and asks for grace.

DAY 4

We Are Weak and Limited

But we have this treasure in jars of clay, to show that the surpassing power belongs to God and not to us. We are afflicted in every way, but not crushed; perplexed, but not driven to despair; persecuted, but not forsaken; struck down, but not destroyed; always carrying in the body the death of Jesus, so that the life of Jesus may also be manifested in our bodies. (2 Cor. 4:7–10)

MANY OF OUR anxieties spring from our daily weakness and our limitations as humans. The Bible recognizes that we are weak, but it points us to a hopeful and perhaps surprising reason for this. In today's verses, the apostle describes circumstances that are filled with great stress while also reminding himself of the purposeful working of God's power within him. Read them again.

Christians are jars of clay; we are common vessels—earthen pots. People who live with disabilities may be more acutely aware of this truth, but all of us experience infirmity. Yet within us dwells something else—the hope that is found in Jesus Christ. This *treasure*—the gospel—takes up residence in weak, fallen people who know that they need the Lord. Our neediness means that "the life of Jesus may also be manifested" through us. Since our struggles provide opportunities for us to glorify God, we may welcome our weakness as we train (and retrain) ourselves to cling to the promise of his enduring presence.

The psalmist reminds us that "the LORD . . . knows our frame; he remembers that we are dust" (Ps. 103:13–14). God knows our weaknesses. Why? Because he made us this way—out of dirt. He engineered confines into our "hardware" (our bodies) and "software" (our souls) to train us to rely on *his* sufficiency, not on our imaginary self-sufficiency. He did this so that we would crave life beyond this life: eternal life with him.

Yet Jesus did not come to provide only eternal life. He came that we also "may have life and have it abundantly" in the here-and-now (John 10:10). The hope that we have in Christ cannot be extinguished. We don't have to succumb to the slave driver named *anxiety*. There is an *inner peace* available from Jesus that is found nowhere else: "Peace I leave with you; my peace I give to you. Not as the world gives do I give to you. Let not your hearts be troubled, neither let them be afraid" (John 14:27).

We are embodied spirits who have weaknesses and limitations. We will continue to be so until death, when our spirits will vacate our weakening shells. Until then, the Lord will help us learn to fight the fear and inner restlessness that we call *anxiety*, by laying hold of our future hope. One day, at the resurrection, we will receive new and imperishable bodies that will leave all our weaknesses behind (see 1 Cor. 15:52).

Do you welcome or reject your weaknesses? Consider how the life of Jesus can be made manifest in your struggles even now.

Reflect: As you embrace your weaknesses and limitations, remember that God alone is the Strong One. "The name of the LORD is a strong tower; the righteous man runs into it and is safe" (Prov. 18:10).

Reflect: In what ways have you not respected your limitations? For example, have you committed yourself to too many tasks? Have you overextended yourself financially? What is stressing you out?

Act: Pray this prayer: Heavenly Father, thank you that I am made in weakness—that I am a jar of clay. Help me to respect the limitations that you designed into my mind and body. But thank you, too, that because of the gospel, the mighty life of Jesus lives in me. Help me to walk in dependence on Jesus so that he is made more visible through my life.

DAY 5

Disordered Worship

"No one can serve two masters, for either he will hate the one and love the other, or he will be devoted to the one and despise the other. You cannot serve God and money. Therefore I tell you, do not be anxious about your life, what you will eat or what you will drink, nor about your body, what you will put on. Is not life more than food, and the body more than clothing?" (Matt. 6:24–25)

WE HAVE SEEN that we are embodied spirits that God designed to rely on him. God created us to glorify and worship him (see Isa. 43:7; Col. 1:16). He placed a desire within us that, before sin entered the world, naturally drove us toward him. Until sin entered the garden, man's affections were *singularly* devoted to God. But now our human nature is fallen, we live in fallen bodies, and we dwell in a fallen world. Our affections are *divided* between God and earthly attachments. Whatever occupies first place in our hearts at any given moment is what draws our energy, attention, and service.

In our passage for today, Jesus says that it's impossible to serve two masters. We were created to be singular in our worship. If we worship money (and make it a god), then we cannot worship the true God. And if we worship God, we will no longer worship money. *The real estate of the human heart has enough space for only one throne.* But when sin entered the world in the form of unbelief, the heart of man became duplicitous. It is disloyal, and it makes our worship become disordered. That's where anxiety may enter the picture.

According to Jesus, anxiety may be a symptom of worship that has gone amiss. Sometimes our hearts are anxious because we have shifted our allegiance (our trust) back and forth from

God to something else—in this case, money or the things that money can buy (food, drink, clothing, and so on). When we do not trust God without reservation, doubt enters our hearts, and we may become like the "double-minded man" who is unstable (James 1:8). Our hearts are divided, and we sway back and forth. The multiple gods that are competing for our hearts unavoidably produce inner turmoil.

Do you worry about the basic necessities of this life? If not, what gods do demand your allegiance? What things are you worrying about that have taken the place of the Lord in your life?

When we worship the One who created us for his glory, all is well with our souls. But when lingering unbelief shifts our devotion away from the Lord, we become anxious and our hearts are brought out of order. In the coming days, we will look at this more closely.

Reflect: In *How to Worship Jesus Christ*, Joseph Carroll explains the history of the word *worship* and gives its meaning as this: "'to attribute worth to an object.' Worship is the 'worthship' of the one you worship."[1] What is the relation between worship and the things that preoccupy your mind? To what people or possessions have you assigned improper worth and, therefore, improper importance and worship?

Act: In your own words, journal a short paragraph summarizing what you learned in today's devotional and, if needed, a prayer of confession.

DAY 6

Discontent and Coveting

Not that I am speaking of being in need, for I have learned in whatever situation I am to be content. . . . In any and every circumstance, I have learned the secret of facing plenty and hunger, abundance and need. I can do all things through him who strengthens me. (Phil. 4:11–13)

IF A COMMERCIAL doesn't produce at least a tinge of "Oh, I wish I had that" in the viewer, then it's failed in its purpose. But, while advertisers work to *cultivate* discontent, they are not the ones who *create* it. Discontent is already in our hearts—ingrained in our fallen nature. The Bible connects it to *covetousness.*

To covet is "to desire inordinately, to place the object of desire before love and devotion to God."[1] Covetousness is a grave sin that leads to other shades of unbelief (not-so-obvious displays of our lack of trust in God)—including anxiety. We must kill it (see Eph. 5:3; Col. 3:5).

What can covetous discontent look like in your life? You may desire fame and thus be discontent with living under the radar, becoming anxious when you are passed over or not affirmed. You may crave acceptance from peers and thus be dissatisfied with pleasing the Lord, becoming anxious about being rejected for your faith in Christ. You may long to have someone else's body type, hair, nose, smile, and so on, and thus be discontent with how God made you—becoming anxious about being noticed, which may then fuel an unbalanced preoccupation with your physical appearance. You may be discontent with your house, car, job, marriage, children (or lack of them), health, and so on—becoming anxious when you don't get the raise you were expecting or when you hear about stock market dips or the rising cost of healthcare.

Regardless of what your discontent looks like or what it

motivates you to do, only God, through your relationship with his Son, can satisfy your heart.

The apostle Paul came to this realization. His testimony is simple: "I count everything as loss because of the surpassing worth of knowing Christ Jesus my Lord" (Phil. 3:8). A relationship with Jesus is the spring from which the pure water of today's verses flows. In them we find two essential truths.

First, *contentment must be learned*. It is not a natural quality but a learned habit. Paul knew what it was like to wonder where his next meal or rent payment would come from. But by God's grace he learned to be at peace "in any and every circumstance." What about us? We get worried about every hard thing in our lives. Contentment, in contrast, is that calm, sweet sense of "enough" that governs our souls when we wholly trust God as our provider.

Second, *Christ is the secret to contentment*. The apostle was not referring to playing football when he said, "I can do all things through him who strengthens me." His school was a prison cell! He had every reason to be anxious. But he also had the best teacher of all. The indwelling Holy Spirit trained Paul to center his joy on the Lord Jesus.

By following the apostle's example, we too can learn to be content. No matter our circumstances, we learn contentment and fight off anxiety by centering our lives on Christ. When we know Jesus and consider him our all-in-all, we find the rest that our anxious hearts need.

Reflect: How might your anxiety be connected to your heart cravings (i.e., how might discontent be feeding your anxiety)?

Act: In your journal, list the things that you crave and why you crave them. Pray through this list. Submit your legitimate needs or wants to the Lord and confess any desires that are disorderly. Ask the Lord to teach you contentment in Christ.

DAY 7

Wicked Envy

Whom have I in heaven but you? And there is nothing on earth that I desire besides you. My flesh and my heart may fail, but God is the strength of my heart and my portion forever. (Ps. 73:25–26)

CONTENTMENT COMES WHEN we center our lives on Christ. Envy comes when we compare ourselves to others who are "better off." Envy easily leads us to doubt God's goodness and to become fearful. That's what happened to Asaph—a skilled musician and worship leader who was appointed by King David (see 1 Chron. 6:39; Ezra 2:41) and was the author of Psalm 73. Asaph knew that "God is good" (Ps. 73:1), but he allowed his heart to doubt this truth because he became "envious" when he "saw the prosperity of the wicked" (v. 3). The rest of this psalm describes his internal wrestling and illustrates the stark contrast between envy and contentment.

Envy looks around (vv. 3–15). Asaph's gaze had zoomed in on the smooth sailing of the wicked, who were getting richer by the day (see v. 12). As a result, he questioned the value of his own godliness: "All in vain have I kept my heart clean" (v. 13). Nothing seemed to go wrong for the wicked. They had "no pangs until death" (v. 4). They were "not in trouble as others are . . . like the rest of mankind" (v. 5). The more he compared his difficult situation to the trouble-free existence of the proud who mocked God (see vv. 6, 11), the more his perspective became distorted and his heart disillusioned.

Faith looks upward and forward (vv. 16–28). The turning point came when Asaph looked to the Lord and to the guarantee of his promises. Previously, when he had tried to make sense of the unfairness, it seemed "a wearisome task" (v. 16). But then something changed. He "went into the sanctuary of God" and "discerned their end" (v. 17). He confessed that his "soul was embittered" (v. 21) and that he was angry at God (see v. 22). When he humbly entered the Lord's presence, Asaph's interpretation of life became clear. He began to understand that God will judge the wicked in his own time and manner. The reward for those who love God is also sure—it just won't be fully realized until eternity. To this day, Asaph's testimony endures: "You guide me with your counsel, and afterward you will receive me to glory" (v. 24).

Today's Scripture depicts the renewed affirmation of Asaph's heart. In heaven, nothing will matter but the Lord. So also, "nothing on earth" holds Asaph's heart any longer. There is nothing that he desires "besides you." This is Asaph's new perspective, as he stands in the sanctuary worshipping with God's people. God alone is his source of strength and ultimate satisfaction. Knowing the Lord is his surpassing treasure. There is no need for him to envy the wicked if, in the end, Asaph will be near God—his true refuge (see v. 28).

God-centered faith breeds contentment of spirit, since it looks not to temporal security but to the fulfillment of God's plan in eternity. It follows God's counsel now while also placing its hope in future glory.

Reflect: The lines between envy, discontent, and anxiety are sometimes thin—they are not easy to see. Working backward from your anxiety, do you see evidence of discontent or envy in your heart?

Reflect: Ask the Lord for the strength to fight your envy, and confess that envy to a mature Christian friend. "Let not your heart envy sinners, but continue in the fear of the LORD all the day" (Prov. 23:17).

Act: Write Psalm 73:25–26 on a 3x5 card and review it often.

DAY 8

Perfectionism May Cause Anxiety

*Since we have been justified by faith, we have peace with God
through our Lord Jesus Christ. Through him we have also
obtained access by faith into this grace in which we stand, and
we rejoice in hope of the glory of God. (Rom. 5:1–2)*

HAS PERFECTIONISM BECOME the enemy of your inner peace? The heart of a perfectionist is never fully at rest. There's always something more for perfectionists to achieve or improve. Striving becomes their pattern of life. And that striving often breeds anxiety. The pursuit of excellence may be a perfectionist's lifelong friend, basing the motivation for his or her diligent work ethic on performance.[1] Perfectionists may fear personal failure or the disappointment of others. They may be stuck in a works-righteousness mindset and thus never feel fully accepted by God.

Regardless of what triggers our unrest, the remedy for it is the same. In Romans 5:1–2, the apostle repeats the words "we have" three times in order to remind us of what is *already* true for believers—what we already possess in Christ. These three assertions of what "we have" show us that we build our experiential peace (the peace *of* God) on the foundation of our relational peace (our peace *with* God).

First, *we have been justified*. To be justified means to be declared righteous by God. In the courtroom of heaven, the status of the repentant sinner who turns to Jesus is changed from "guilty" to "righteous." In exchange for our sin, Jesus gives us his perfect righteousness (see 2 Cor. 5:21). This is all received "by faith"—it is not gained through the perfection of our works.

Second, *we have peace with God*. Having been declared righteous by God, we change from being enemies of God into being children of God. Peace with God is not something we work *for* but something we work *from*, since Jesus is already "our peace" (Eph. 2:14). Acceptance with God is not gained through our spiritual performance; it is based on Christ's perfect righteousness—not ours. God "made us accepted in the Beloved" one—Christ (Eph. 1:6 NKJV).

Third, *we have access to God.* Our permission to enter God's presence is also "by faith"—not by works. Through Christ we have access "into this grace in which we [already] stand." We enter the throne room of God based on his grace, not on our prior or current spiritual performance. This gift of grace is the righteousness of his sinless Son (see Rom. 5:17). We can enter the presence of God only because Jesus first offered himself as the once-for-all sacrifice (see Heb. 10:10, 19–20).

When we renew our minds with these truths, "we rejoice in hope of the glory of God" (Rom. 5:2). Thinking about what Jesus has already done for us breeds contentment, corrects our perfectionism, and retrains us to place greater confidence in the finished work of Christ than in our unfinished works. In short, truth feeds joy, which combats anxiety.

The next time anxiety strikes, don't focus on what's going wrong and on what you need to get done. Rather, fix your gaze on Christ and on his gift of righteousness to us. Because of the grace of Christ, there is no reason for us to be anxious.

Reflect: Do you see perfectionism in your life? In what ways?

Act: Read Proverbs 29:25. How can pleasing people become a trap? What is the opposite of pleasing people?

Act: Meditate on Psalm 127:2. We are called to be diligent— but is it possible to work too hard? What might overwork reveal about your faith?

DAY 9

Anger, Irritability, and Frustration

Martha was distracted by all the preparations that had to be made. She came to him and asked, "Lord, don't you care that my sister has left me to do the work by myself? Tell her to help me!" "Martha, Martha," the Lord answered, "you are worried and upset about many things." (Luke 10:40–41 NIV)

THERE IS A fine line between anxiety and anger. And when we cross this line, we often excuse it as *irritability* or *frustration*. But could something more be going on? Anxiety often results in our being annoyed with people who don't appear to be as concerned as we are, and this annoyance typically spawns other sins in turn.

This is the case with Martha, as we witness her being distracted by the cares that spring from having a guest in her home. Luke sets the stage: "A woman named Martha welcomed [Jesus] into her house. And she had a sister called Mary, who sat at the Lord's feet and listened to his teaching" (Luke 10:38–39). Martha is forever remembered for her hospitable spirit . . . and for being preoccupied with the *tasks* that were associated with her hospitality rather than with the *person* to whom she was being hospitable.

Mary knew whose presence she was in, and she cherished every moment that she had with her Savior. So she "sat at the Lord's feet and listened to his teaching." Martha, however, "was distracted by all the preparations that had to be made." At first, Martha kept her emotions in check. But when her anxiety conceived annoyance, it gave birth to an angry response.

We typically recognize Martha's displeasure with her sister but miss the deeper issue behind it. Martha vented her frustration at Jesus: "Lord, don't you care . . . ?" Martha was uptight about Mary's seeming lack of concern for "the important stuff"—i.e., Martha's to-do list. But her inward focus made its presence known outwardly when she took it out on Jesus. She accused him of lacking compassion or personal care for her and commanded the Son of God (think about that!) to tell her sister to get busy.

But Jesus responds with such patience: "Martha, Martha . . . you are worried and upset about many things." He does not harshly rebuke her but gently corrects her. He helps her to discern the source of her anxiety: her preoccupation with lesser things. Only "one thing is necessary," Jesus says. "Mary has chosen the good portion, which will not be taken away from her" (Luke 10:42). Martha's anxiety caused her to miss out on spending time with the most important visitor ever to grace her home!

Emotions are not neutral or amoral. They are either godly or ungodly—self-centered or God-centered. Physical or medical considerations notwithstanding, there is always something going on in our hearts in relation to God when we experience anxiety. We are never fully passive, but our hearts (our control centers) are always active—always choosing between the lesser and the greater. Martha chose her to-do list over Jesus. When your anxiety is provoked, what do you choose?

Reflect: How do you see your anxiety leading to other sins?

Reflect: How does your anxiety distract you from spending time with Jesus?

Act: Write a confession to God, admitting the lesser things that distract you from Christ.

TURNING TO GOD IN OUR ANXIETY

DAY 10

In the Pasture of the Good Shepherd

"I am the good shepherd. I know my own and my own know me, just as the Father knows me and I know the Father; and I lay down my life for the sheep." (John 10:14–15)

THE HOLY SPIRIT brings us assurance as we meditate on the love Jesus shows for sinners. I'm not referring to his *former* demonstration of love, which he showed by dying in our place, but to his *perpetual* love in the here and now. Jesus is not only our Lord and Savior but also our faithful Good Shepherd. Focusing on this reality will bring you peace and security in your most anxious moments.

Jesus's description of himself in today's passage highlights the shepherding care that he provides to those who dwell in his pasture. From this chapter of John emerge four assurances.

The Good Shepherd laid down his life for you. When Jesus said, "The good shepherd lays down his life for the sheep" (v. 11), his death was still in the future—he *would* lay down his life for them. But that is done now. His sin-bearing work is complete. Sin has been punished. Your debt has already been paid in full (see Heb. 9:27–28). By consciously remembering this ultimate demonstration of love, you will further assure your heart of Jesus's ongoing love and care today . . . and every day . . . into eternity.

The Good Shepherd will not leave you. Jesus is unlike others. "He who is a hired hand and not a shepherd . . . sees the wolf coming and leaves the sheep and flees" (John 10:12). Your faithful Shepherd stays by your side when wolves attack. He will never abandon you (see Heb. 13:5). He will never desert you or leave you to the greatest enemy of your soul—Satan.

The Good Shepherd is committed to you. The hired hand "cares nothing for the sheep" (John 10:13). The hireling flees because he is self-concerned, but Jesus demonstrates his love by leading you with his staff and training you with his rod. Christ's commitment to his sheep is found not in empty words but in deep promises.

The Good Shepherd knows you, in relationship, just as he knows the Father in relationship. Jesus knows those who are his own, and those who are his own know him. "I am the good shepherd. I know my own and my own know me, just as the Father knows me and I know the Father" (vv. 14–15). Christ's relationship with his Father is the deepest and most intimate relationship in the entire universe. Jesus likens his relationship with you to his relationship with the Father. Encouraging, isn't it? Growing in Christ is more than gaining Bible knowledge. It includes developing a closeness with your Shepherd, as you listen to his Word and follow him by faith.

As your worries bombard your heart and mind, don't give in to them. Instead, turn to Jesus. Your Good Shepherd awaits. He loves and cares for those who repent and who believe in his saving name (see Acts 4:12). As you deliberately set your anxious mind on these truths, you will find your heart resting securely in his love.

Reflect: How does thinking about Jesus's love for you, and about his desire to have fellowship with you, influence your desire to know him more?

Reflect: What can you do today to nurture your relationship with the Lord?

Act: Read Hebrews 13:20–21. Journal the comforting truths that you discover there about Jesus, the Good Shepherd. Compare your findings with what Psalm 23 says about the Shepherd.

DAY 11

"Come to Me, and I Will
Give You Rest"

*"Come to me, all who labor and are heavy laden, and I will give
you rest. Take my yoke upon you, and learn from me, for I am
gentle and lowly in heart, and you will find rest for your souls. For
my yoke is easy, and my burden is light." (Matt. 11:28–30)*

REST IS THE polar opposite of anxiety. Our anxious hearts
long for rest but can't seem to find it. And the rest that we need
is even deeper than the rest that we typically seek. Too often, we
crave immediate relief from our worry rather than the ultimate
respite: the quiet contentment for our souls that is found in Jesus.
The antidote to our anxiety is *security in the Savior*.

What is the context for today's verses? Jesus's command
"Come to me" immediately follows a bold revelation of his deity
and of his intimate fellowship with the Father (see Matt. 11:25–
27). Jesus then connects the rest that we seek from our present
burdens to the all-important rest that is found in him.

Consider three truths from Matthew 11:28–30 that enable us
to rest.

Jesus commands all who are burdened to come to him (v. 28).
The adjective "heavy laden" refers to being burdened by a mas-
sive weight of great importance. Since the context of this verse
reveals that Jesus's immediate audience is unbelievers, the burden
of greatest importance that he is referring to must be sin. As the
"one mediator between God and men" (1 Tim. 2:5), he is in the
rightful position to command us to come to him. The Bible calls
repenting of unbelief and believing in Christ "the obedience of
faith" (Rom. 1:5). By faith we cease whatever religious "labor" we

think may earn our salvation, and we rest in the finished work of our gentle, but triumphant, Savior.

Jesus commands us to be learners (v. 29). When we obey the gospel's call to come to the Lord Jesus for salvation from our sin, we become disciples—learners. We become lifelong apprentices of Jesus as we carry his yoke. But Jesus says that this yoke is "easy" and that the "burden" of obedience is "light"—just as the apostle John teaches: the commandments of Jesus "are not burdensome" (1 John 5:3).

Jesus promises "soul rest" (v. 29–30). The ultimate rest that Jesus promises to all who come to him is peace for their souls. The burden of sin's penalty is completely lifted, and we are forgiven. But Christ never promises complete deliverance from life's other burdens, trials, and afflictions. He promises the exact opposite to his disciples—that they will be persecuted and hated because of him (see John 15:18–19). Nonetheless, Jesus promises to carry these burdens with us and for us.

The stubborn root of anxiety is a fundamental distrust in God's sovereignty, love, and goodness to us—as though Christ doesn't matter anymore. We must sever the root of unbelief at its deepest point by applying the gospel, which is "the power of God for salvation to everyone who believes" (Rom. 1:16). If we are yoked to Jesus, then nothing that we might fear can threaten God's love for us. Nothing (see Rom. 8:38–39). Now that's what I call *rest!*

Reflect: What words would you use to describe your soul's rest in Jesus? Are there any burdens of sin that you have not confessed to God?

Act: Write a prayer to Jesus. Humbly acknowledge that sometimes your anxiety is the result of your attempt to carry burdens that he already carries, and thank him for the lightness of his yoke.

DAY 12

Your Heavenly Father Cares

"Look at the birds of the air: they neither sow nor reap nor gather into barns, and yet your heavenly Father feeds them. Are you not of more value than they? And which of you by being anxious can add a single hour to his span of life?" (Matt. 6:26–27)

FAKE CARES ARE problems that our fears dream up. They exist only in our imagination. Since God has promised to meet our needs, to continue to worry about them *not* being met is to create a care that isn't a real threat. Such fake cares steal mental real estate and emotional energy from us by creating distractions.

In today's verses, Jesus says that we should not worry about what is not ours to worry about. Instead, we should be more like the birds, which do not doubt the faithfulness of God. When we intentionally "look at the birds," we remind ourselves of how dependent all creatures are—and especially ourselves. As we wait on the Lord, our responsibility is to actively do what he commands and to leave the rest to him.

Worry distracts us from enjoying the love of our heavenly Father, but Jesus offers us comforting truths to settle our anxious hearts.

Your heavenly Father feeds his creatures (v. 26). God cares for the things he creates. He takes responsibility for them. Jesus directs us to look at the birds—to consider how their needs are faithfully met. They own no barns and have no ability to store up for the future. Yet God meets their daily needs.

You are more valuable than any non-human creature (v. 27). Jesus also reassures us that we are infinitely more valuable than animals are. Human life possesses fathomless value because man and woman are created in God's image and likeness. We are designed to reflect God's glory. This is what gives human beings their worth.

Your heavenly Father has a plan for the span of your life (v. 27). When King David praised God for the wonder-filled way he had created him, he also acknowledged that God would providentially lead him according to his sovereign plan. "In your book were written, every one of them, the days that were formed for me, when as yet there was none of them," he testified (Ps. 139:16). Since this is true for each of us, worrying about tomorrow will not "add a single hour to [the] span of [our] life."

God faithfully provides for us. He does this primarily through our work and through our disciplined stewardship of our resources (see Prov. 6:6–11). Nevertheless, even if we are faithful with our responsibilities and resources, we may have needs that remain unmet. If this is the case for us, then we trust God to provide for us in his way and according to his timetable. To fret is to heap fake cares on our large-enough stack of legitimate ones.

Reflect: What are your fake cares? List them, and also review your "care list" from day 1. Are the items you are currently worrying about legitimate cares, or could some be things that you fear *might* happen?

Act: If you can't distinguish between fake and true cares, turn to a wise Christian friend and ask for help.

Act: Read Psalm 127:2. Compare it to what Jesus teaches about the heavenly Father's care and provision.

DAY 13

Your Heavenly Father Provides

*"But if God so clothes the grass of the field, which today is
alive and tomorrow is thrown into the oven, will he not much
more clothe you, O you of little faith?" (Matt. 6:30)*

WE ARE EARTHBOUND people who naturally focus on
earthly burdens. Our smallness of faith exposes itself in our pre-
disposition to worry about our needs instead of resting in the care
that our Creator promises. Our faith is not yet fully grown; it con-
tinually needs to be nurtured. Knowing that this is the case, Jesus
develops our faith by gently confronting our unbelief.

In the verses that precede our verse for today, Jesus employs
another image from nature to ask a conscience-stirring question.
"Why are you anxious about clothing? Consider [i.e., deliberately
notice] the lilies of the field, how they grow: they neither toil nor
spin" (Matt. 6:28). Clearly he intends to redirect weary eyes of
faith to look godward.

Jesus directs us to think about how the flowers are clothed.
They do not buy or spin their own fabric. They are beautifully
adorned by the Lord—such that "even Solomon in all his glory
was not arrayed like one of these" (Matt. 6:29). Jesus does *not* dis-
courage us from working hard in order to provide for ourselves.
But no matter how hard we can possibly work, God is always working harder on our behalf. He is the ultimate provider. If God cares
for the flowers and dresses them in a dazzling array of shapes and
colors, and if he clothes the grass of the field—which is destined
to be destroyed—with such a lovely array of these flowers, how
much *more* does he care for *you*. We must acknowledge his tender
care and trust him with our concerns—for, as Jesus asserts, "your
Father knows what you need before you ask him" (Matt. 6:8).

This faithful care should produce great confidence in a believer. In light of this, Jesus relates anxiety to having "little faith." The root of our anxiety is unbelief. He challenges unbelief and the small view of God that it takes—the fact that when we are anxious, we fear that God is lacking. But God is not deficient in any virtue. Nor is he ever unfaithful.

In all these questions and exhortations, Jesus is saying the same thing over and over. "Look at what God is doing. Look at the flowers. Look at the grass. God takes constant care of them, and they are temporal. He tends to their needs. Why do you not trust God when you are infinitely more valuable and will live for eternity?" Unbelief and anxiety both whisper in your ear, "Your needs won't be met. What are you going to do?" In our fight against anxiety, a small view of God will never suffice. God delegated the care of the earth to man (see Gen. 2:15), but he has always been the Gardener. And the pinnacle of God's creation is man (see Ps. 8). Therefore, believe that God will meet your needs. Have faith. God cares about you!

Reflect: How does your view of God impact your trust in him? How does it help you to fight your anxiety?

Act: Meditate on Jeremiah 17:7–8. Journal about the fruit of trusting God. Write these verses on a 3x5 card. Read them often. Let their truth remind you to turn your gaze upward.

Act: Find a wise Christian friend and share with him or her how you have seen God meet your needs. Then, together, praise the Lord for how he cares for you.

DAY 14

Your Heavenly Father Knows

"Therefore do not be anxious, saying, 'What shall we eat?'
or 'What shall we drink?' or 'What shall we wear?' For the
Gentiles seek after all these things, and your heavenly Father
knows that you need them all." (Matt. 6:31–32)

IN TODAY'S PASSAGE, Jesus brings up a relationship that
unbelievers (Gentiles) do not have. They worry about the basic
necessities—food, drink, clothing. But we have spiritual blessings that far outweigh material ones as well as a confidence that
cannot belong to the non-Christian. Through our repentant faith
in Christ, *the* heavenly Father has become *our* heavenly Father. He
takes care of the animal and plant kingdoms, and he loves his children infinitely more (see Matt. 6:25–30). Therefore, we should
not be anxious (see v. 31). We have no need to worry about our
basic provisions (see v. 32). What supports this confidence in
our heavenly Father's personal care is the gospel. The redemptive
work that Jesus completed to deliver us from the penalty of sin
also rescues us from the orphanage of the Evil One and places us
into the family of God.

We were not always his children. Before we were born again,
we were "children of wrath, like the rest of mankind" (Eph. 2:3).
We were God's enemies (see Rom. 5:10; Col. 1:21). But when
God opened our hearts to the gospel and we believed in Jesus, we
were set free from the penalty and power of sin. God "delivered us
from the domain of darkness and transferred us to the kingdom
of his beloved Son" (Col. 1:13). His amazing grace initiated our
adoption as children of God (see Gal. 4:4–5).

Spiritual adoption is the gracious act of God by which he
places the believer in Jesus into his family and gives him the full

rights and privileges of mature sonship. In light of this adoption, the apostle Paul explains why we should not be controlled by fear: "For you did not receive the spirit of slavery to fall back into fear, but you have received the Spirit of adoption as sons" (Rom. 8:15). Unlike unbelievers, you have a heavenly Father whom you can turn to—one who knows and cares.

This secure relationship should produce in you a peaceful, trusting disposition—one that is different from those who do not have God as their Father. This is the basis of Jesus's directive "Do not be anxious." Children of God can rest in the promise that our Father has made to meet our every need, but "Gentiles [unbelievers] seek after all these things." Our relationship with God should lead us to have heavenly priorities and a distinct outlook that is unbound by anxiety. Because you are God's, you don't have to worry. As pastor Philip De Courcy says, "Anxious care, or illegitimate concern, is out of place in the company of Christians and certainly in the presence of God."[1] When our hearts settle into the reality that the God of the universe is our very own, personal heavenly Father, there is no longer a need for us to be anxious. He knows our every need and will provide for us.

Do you know God as your heavenly Father—and, if so, what difference is that making in your life? Does it help you to no longer worry?

Reflect: Why and how is anxiety not God's will for you as a Christian?

Act: Read Romans 8:15–17. Journal about the blessings of adoption in Christ.

Act: Write a personal prayer to your heavenly Father. Thank him for adopting you and for promising to meet your needs.

FIGHTING ANXIETY

DAY 15

Choose to Rejoice

Rejoice in the Lord always; again I will say, rejoice. Let your reasonableness be known to everyone. (Phil. 4:4–5)

"I WANT HAPPINESS," a friend told me. He's one of many people I know who want to be happy and yet often look for happiness in the wrong places. As I write this chapter, Amazon's search engine produces over fifty thousand results for books about happiness. Yet even with all this self-help available, people are chronically unhappy.

For example, pervasive unhappiness is seen in the form of negativity in the workplace. *Forbes* magazine recently published an article stating that "disengaged employees are the norm" and that "where there are disengaged employees, there's usually complaining, gossiping, and griping." The author continues, "Whether you occasionally struggle with a victim mentality or have had your fair share of true bad breaks, it's reassuring to remember that when it comes to your own behavior, you hold all the power and you always have a choice."[1]

"You always have a choice." Did you catch that? And that's counsel from a *secular* magazine. How much more should a scriptural exhortation grab our attention!

Philippians 4:4–5 make up a *command* from God. Consider the two admonitions that are given and their connection to each other.

- *Rejoice in the Lord at all times.* This directive for the congregation in Philippi continues the theme of the epistle overall: rejoicing (see Phil. 1:18; 2:17–18, 28; 3:1). Biblical joy is both a *feeling*—an unanticipated emotional response to something wonderful—as well as an *action* that can be commanded.[2] Keep in mind that Paul is in prison awaiting the outcome of his trial when he exhorts us to rejoice at all times. He demonstrates firsthand how we must choose to look to the Lord as our ultimate source of joy. In other words, true joy is not dependent on our circumstances. Lasting joy is found only *in the Lord.*

- *Let your gentleness be evident to all people.* The word *reasonableness* in verse 5 may also be translated *gentleness. Gentleness* fits well, since it is a preeminent characteristic of Christ—the one in whom we are called to rejoice. There's only one point in all four gospels when Jesus describes his humanity in personal terms. It's when he says, "I am gentle and lowly in heart" (Matt. 11:29). Gentleness is a Christlike quality. When our joy and gentleness are "known to everyone," we draw attention to Jesus. Whether you choose to rejoice or complain, your choice impacts your witness.

But what do joy and gentleness have to do with anxiety?

Anxiety is a joy-killer. It feeds on, and often exaggerates, actual problems or potential negative outcomes. The resulting inner agitation that we feel undermines our calm and gentleness. But, as Christ-followers, we should not be known for a negative spirit; we should be known for a peaceful, hopeful spirit. This Christlike demeanor is within our reach, because it begins with a choice—the choice to rejoice.

Reflect: Do you have the tendency to let circumstances be the basis of your joy (or your lack of it)? Why is that?

Act: In your journal, list reasons why you should rejoice in the Lord.

DAY 16

Worry about Nothing; Pray about Everything

The Lord is at hand; do not be anxious about anything, but in everything by prayer and supplication with thanksgiving let your requests be made known to God. (Phil. 4:5–6)

TODAY'S SCRIPTURE CONTAINS a twofold command: be anxious about nothing but prayerful about everything. Notice, though, that this charge is preceded by the promise that "the Lord is at hand." When we rejoice in the Lord, our focus shifts off our troubles and onto the promise of our Lord's triumphant return.

First, since the Lord is near, we are told, "Do not be anxious about anything"—present, future, or past.

Is it possible to worry about our past? For sure. It's called *regret*. Martyn Lloyd-Jones wrote, "The past cannot be recalled and you can do nothing about it. You can sit down and be miserable and you can go round and round in circles of regret for the rest of your life but it will make no difference to what you have done. . . . We must never for a second worry about anything that cannot be affected or changed by us. It is a waste of energy."[1]

Sometimes we waste a lot of time and energy worrying about our past failures. But if we have repented and sought forgiveness from God—and from other people, where possible (see Rom. 12:18)—we need to be actively "forgetting what lies behind and straining forward to what lies ahead" (Phil. 3:13). Whether we are faced with regrets over the past, the pressures of today, or worries about the future, we should not be anxious about anything.

Second, we are told to bring everything to God. Paul explains *four different aspects* of what prayer includes, through four words that he uses in verse 6.

Worship God. The word *prayer* refers to calling on God as part of our worship. The more we pray about everything, the more we consciously submit our lives to the Lord. The more we worry, the more we trust our own ability to control things—or even people. As a result, we often end up worshiping our hearts' idols—whatever makes us feel safe or in control.

Cry out to God. The second aspect of praying about everything is bringing all our needs to God, because he's fully able to meet them. *Supplication* implies that we have been provoked by the realization that we lack something essential. In prayer, we bring our needs to God—not because he is unaware but because we need to acknowledge our dependence on him.

Always be grateful. We should pray with *thanksgiving.* Pray to God *while* also being thankful—*with* an attitude of gratitude. Thanksgiving is a key to gaining victory over our anxiety, since it deliberately shifts our heart's eye from our current worries to the mighty works of God.

Verbalize your specific needs. "Let your *requests* be made known to God." The Father knows our needs, but many times he does not meet them unless we pray for them, because we need the humility that prayer effects in us.

By thinking about these four aspects, we understand how God uses prayer as part of his prescription for anxiety. God calls us to worship him through prayer and invites us to make our needs known and to bring specific requests to him in a spirit of dependence and thanksgiving.

Reflect: When you become anxious, how quickly do you turn to the Lord in prayer?

Reflect: Amid your present concerns, what can you thank God for?

Act: List your top three worries and then pray about them.

DAY 17

Find Peace through Prayer

And the peace of God, which surpasses all understanding, will
guard your hearts and your minds in Christ Jesus. (Phil. 4:7)

GOD WANTS US to bring everything to him in prayer, because
we need the humility and dependence that prayer effects in us
(see Phil. 4:5–6). As the result of our prayer, the peace of God
protects our hearts and minds from fear, as we see in today's verse.
God's peace commands our anxious thoughts to leave and pre-
vents new ones from entering. This inner peace has three qualities.

First, *it is an indescribable calm.* This peace eludes adequate
description—it "surpasses all understanding." It is a peace that
the world cannot understand or furnish. Jesus says, "Peace I leave
with you; my peace I give to you. Not as the world gives do I
give to you. Let not your hearts be troubled, neither let them be
afraid" (John 14:27).

Second, *it protects emotional and mental stability.* The apostle
assures us that this peace "will guard your hearts and your minds."
The word *guard* is a military word. It refers to a garrison of sol-
diers on duty. When we pray, God dispatches a defense force of
armed warriors to surround our inner person and protect it from
anxiety attacks that would disturb our peace. This reminds us of
a wonderful promise: "You [i.e., the Lord] keep him in perfect
peace whose mind is stayed on you, because he trusts in you" (Isa.
26:3). When our attention is fixed on the Lord, his peace watches
over our hearts and minds.

Third, *it belongs to believers only.* This peace guards the hearts
and minds of those who are "in Christ Jesus." To be "in Christ"
means to be united to him by faith (see Gal. 2:20).[1] Only when
we are connected to Jesus can his peace reign in our hearts. This

indescribable calm cannot be experienced by the unsaved person, because it comes from the Holy Spirit (see Gal. 5:22).

If you are not at peace *with* God, you will never be able to experience the peace *of* God. Being at peace with God means that your sins have justly been dealt with on the cross of Calvary (see 1 Peter 3:18). It means that you trust in Jesus Christ as your crucified and risen Lord and Savior who has made peace with God for you (see Col. 1:20). He is the only Mediator between God and sinners (see 1 Tim. 2:5). When you come to God through faith in his Son and receive his atoning work on your behalf, then this rock-solid promise belongs to you: "Since we have been justified by faith, we have peace with God through our Lord Jesus Christ" (Rom. 5:1). Are you at peace with God? If not, you cannot even begin to overcome anxiety. Spiritual peace is found only "in Christ Jesus." If you are not a Christian, turn to Jesus in faith today.

If you already know Jesus Christ, then rest in the peace that God has provided. Those who are redeemed by the blood of the Lamb find security in his promise: "In me you may have peace. In the world you will have tribulation. But take heart; I have overcome the world" (John 16:33).

Reflect: How does being at peace *with* God lead to experiencing the peace *of* God?

Act: Go to God in prayer. Confess your anxieties to him. Let him send his peace to set a guard around your heart and post a sign saying, "Anxiety, you are no longer allowed here. Don't disturb the peace!"

Act: Meditate on Isaiah 26:3. Write the verse on a 3x5 card and place it somewhere you will see it often—or perhaps put it on a note in your smartphone.

DAY 18

Think Positive

Whatever is true, whatever is honorable, whatever is just, whatever is pure, whatever is lovely, whatever is commendable, if there is any excellence, if there is anything worthy of praise, think about these things. (Phil. 4:8)

WHAT YOU THINK about matters. It matters a lot. Think for a minute about how important it is to think about your thinking.

- Prior to being born again, your way of thinking was futile and your understanding darkened (see Eph. 4:17–18).
- At the new birth you received the Holy Spirit, who knows the mind of God (see 1 Cor. 2:11).
- The Spirit thus revealed God's thoughts to you through the Scriptures (see 1 Cor. 2:12–16).
- As a new creature in Christ (see 2 Cor. 5:17), you are personally responsible to put off the old self, which includes your natural way of thinking, and to be renewed in the spirit of your mind (Eph. 4:22–23).
- As you renew your mind with scriptural truth, your life is transformed—which results in your fulfilling the will of God (Rom 12:1–2).

To sum it up, in Christ you have every resource necessary for developing a Christian mind.

Yet what do our minds do when anxiety hits? Our worries trap us in a prison of negative thinking. "What if I don't get that raise?" "What if my health goes downhill?" "What if my son doesn't convert?" "What if I don't finish my work on time?" "What if he never opens up to me?" We are plagued with these thoughts, and anxiety fuels our minds to run down ungodly paths. What worrisome thoughts are you wrestling with now?

Here is Paul's answer to this problem: "If there is any excellence, if there is anything worthy of praise, think about these things" (Phil. 4:8). Don't let the "if" throw you off; the verse isn't saying, "*If* excellent things exist, *then* . . ." Sometimes the word *if* has the sense of meaning "because" or "since." *Because* excellent and praiseworthy virtues do exist, *then* think about these things. That's Paul's point—he commands us to set our minds on the redemptive qualities that are vital to Christlike thinking. "Whatever is *true*, what is *honorable*, whatever is *just*, whatever is *pure*, whatever is *lovely*, whatever is *commendable* . . ."

On many days, this may feel futile. But, by God's strength and through the work of the Spirit in you, you can fight your way out of the prison of negative thinking. God can supernaturally help you to fight the negative thoughts. Do you believe this to be true?

At the same time, you have a responsibility to "think about these things." Don't give in to your worries. As we saw yesterday, the peace of God that results from prayer can guard your heart and mind from fear (see Phil. 4:7). Then you can grab hold of these excellent and praiseworthy things and focus your mind rather than letting it be overrun with fear.

Are you up for this challenge—to focus your mind on the right things?

Reflect: When you are anxious, what negative thoughts commonly occupy your mind?

Reflect: Each of the virtues that are mentioned in Philippians 4:8 are fulfilled perfectly in Christ. For example, Jesus said, "I am the way, and *the truth*, and the life" (John 14:6).

Act: Create a "think positive" chart in your journal. In the left column, list negative thoughts. In the right column, list contrasting positive truths that are based on Scripture.

DAY 19

Cultivate an Attitude of Gratitude

*And let the peace of Christ rule in your hearts, to which indeed
you were called in one body. And be thankful. Let the word of
Christ dwell in you richly, teaching and admonishing one another
in all wisdom, singing psalms and hymns and spiritual songs,
with thankfulness in your hearts to God. (Col. 3:15–16)*

LUKE 17:11–19 TELLS of the time when Jesus healed ten lepers but only one of them returned to show his gratitude. Christ had healed the leper physically—but, much more importantly, our Lord had also healed the leprosy of the sin in his heart. According to Jesus, this man's faith made him "well" (Luke 17:19). What distinguished this man from the other nine? He met Jesus as his Savior, not just as a healer. As a result, he became a new creature in Christ. And his soul-saving encounter produced in him a heart of thankfulness.

The thankful leper's conversion illustrates the new-creature expectation that is found in many New Testament letters—the expectation that sinners saved by grace will be filled with gratitude. The larger context of today's verses is God's command to believers to "put off the old self with its practices" and "put on the new self" (Col. 3:9–10).

Two spiritual disciplines cultivate an attitude of gratitude.

Let the peace of God rule your heart. An attitude of gratitude is directly connected to whether or not the peace of God rules our hearts. As we saw in day 8, having the peace *of* God is different from being at peace *with* God. Peace *with* God is positional—it is related to who we are in Christ. We are no longer enemies but friends, submissive kingdom citizens, and children (see John 15:15; Col. 1:21–22; 1 John 3:2). But the peace *of* God is experiential—it's a calm assurance that guards our inner person through Word-based trust, the Holy Spirit, and prayer (see Isa. 26:3; Rom. 14:17; Phil. 4:6–7). When God's peace rules our hearts, anxiety has a harder time getting in. It's far too easy for us to search for quick fixes to our worries, such as rearranging our circumstances. (Difficult job? Find another one. Difficult relationship? Avoid the other person.) While this may provide us temporary relief, long-lasting *experiential* peace comes from *positional* peace. In order for us to quell our anxieties, we must first be made right with God.

Let the Word of Christ richly dwell within you. Meditating on the Word permits it to sink deeply into our inner person. It challenges and changes our minds' worries and our hearts' fears, which produces joy. This joy then produces a desire in us to sing Christ-exalting praise. It seems clear from this text that a thankful spirit flows from a heart that is touched by grace, controlled by the Spirit, and fed by the Word.

So when we are anxious, we should ask, "What's going on in my heart?" More than likely, we lack the attitude of gratitude that flows from the rule and enrichment of the Word.

Though anxiety and ingratitude are common bedfellows, they should not be a lifestyle for those who know Christ.

Reflect: When do you sing praise to God? Is the Sunday gathering of God's people the only time when you sing psalms, hymns, and spiritual songs? If so, why?

Reflect: What changes do you need to make concerning your intake of the Word through reading, study, and memorization? If you are not sure how to make these changes, find a mature Christian and ask for help.

Act: Begin a "why I'm thankful" list in your journal, and add to it as the Spirit brings to your mind ways in which God's grace has been poured into your life.

DAY 20

Kill Worry with Daggers of Truth

For though we walk in the flesh, we are not waging war according to the flesh. For the weapons of our warfare are not of the flesh but have divine power to destroy strongholds. We destroy arguments and every lofty opinion raised against the knowledge of God, and take every thought captive to obey Christ. (2 Cor. 10:3–5)

WE ARE IN a spiritual war that cannot be fought with non-spiritual weapons. Since this battle lies in mental "strongholds," "arguments," and human opinions, we must fight against the world, the flesh, and the devil in that same realm. To defeat these lies we must take up the sword of the Spirit, which is the Word of God (see Eph. 6:17). We kill doubts and lies with *daggers of truth*—condensed statements that are rooted in biblical teaching.

In order to conquer anxiety, you must learn to consistently slay the lies that your depraved heart believes. Replace worldly conclusions with biblical truth. "Be transformed by the renewal of your mind" (Rom. 12:2). This renewal means washing out your worldly way of thinking "by filling it with a new, fresh supply of God's way of thinking as found in the Scriptures."[1] "Take every thought captive" by bringing it into submission to the Word of God.

Let's meditate again on Jesus's faith-building words concerning God's faithful care (see Matt. 6:25–34). But this time, let's take a different approach. Counsel yourself with the Christ-centered truths below that are based on Jesus's words in this passage. One useful hint: try reading them out loud so that they enter your eyes and ears at the same time.

- God commands me, "Do not be anxious." I need to repent of worry (see vv. 25, 34).

- The essence of life is far more significant than material things (see v. 25).
- Birds don't worry, fret, or hoard, and yet their needs are met (see v. 26).
- God feeds the birds, which are not even made in his image (see v. 26).
- Since I am made in God's image, I am more valuable to him than all the birds in nature (see v. 26).
- Worry will not help me to live longer (see v. 27).
- Flowers are clothed by God. God will clothe me too (see vv. 28–30).
- Worry grows from unbelief—not faith (see v. 30).
- Worry is characteristic of unbelievers and worldly-minded people (see vv. 31–32).
- My heavenly Father knows my needs (see v. 32).
- All my material cares will be taken care of by God when I pursue Christ and his agenda above all (see v. 33).
- Anxiety borrows from tomorrow but never pays back the favor. It only doubles today's trouble (see v. 34).
- Tomorrow has enough trouble of its own. I shouldn't add to it by worrying (see v. 34).

There. That's how to mine a portion of Scripture, pick out nuggets of ore, and forge them into daggers of truth that you can use to kill worry.

Reflect: What doubts or lies commonly feed your struggle with anxiety? Write them down and confess them to the Lord.

Act: You can mine Scripture just like I did. Read Psalm 37. What truth-daggers do you find in this passage that can help you to kill worry? List them in your journal, then pray through them.

DAY 21

Cast Your Cares

Humble yourselves, therefore, under the mighty hand of God so that at the proper time he may exalt you, casting all your anxieties on him, because he cares for you. (1 Peter 5:6–7)

ANXIETY IS SOMETIMES the fruit of pride—especially when it is accompanied by prayerlessness. Though we often minimize our lack of prayer, prayerlessness unmasks an independent spirit—it reveals our failure to recognize our weakness and utter dependence on God. When you don't pray, and when you take on your anxieties by yourself, you show your need for humility before the Lord.

Peter makes this important connection. But notice that before Peter exhorts his readers (who are suffering Christians) to make a habit of bringing their anxieties to God—of throwing them at his feet, so to speak—he issues a call to humility. We must cultivate true humility in ourselves and for ourselves. Like a garment, we must put it on (see Col. 3:12). No human being can do that for us. Yes, others may humiliate us, but only the Spirit's sanctifying work can move us to genuinely humble ourselves. In order to do this, we need divine grace to combat pride and unbelief. Today's verses are loaded with transformative truth for our anxiety-prone hearts. We find a command, its purpose, a manner of obeying the command, and the reason for obeying it.

The command is to humble yourself. Verse 6 begins with "humble yourselves" and is immediately followed by the word "therefore." This command is preceded by a warning and a promise: "God opposes the proud but gives grace to the humble" (v. 5). When you humble yourself before God, he gives you more grace. This grace empowers you to resist allowing anxiety about your trials to push you away from God.

The purpose of humility is to help us to exchange self-exaltation with trust in God. Anxiety is often related to our desire for control, which is connected to thinking too highly of ourselves. Peter's warning is this: If you exalt yourself, you will be humbled by God's mighty hand. But if you humble yourself, the same "mighty hand of God" will exalt you "at the proper time."

The manner of humbling yourself is to cast your cares on God. Peter doesn't simply bark out a command; he tells us specifically how to obey. The way to heed the command to be humble is by "casting all your anxieties" on God. You accomplish this by talking to God and releasing your cares to him by faith. Are you ready to bring your anxieties to the Lord as an act of humility?

The reason to humble yourself in prayer is clear: God cares for you. Peter connects relief from anxiety to an awareness of God's faithful care. "He cares" is in the present tense in the original Greek, referring to continual action. This is Peter's way of stressing how much God constantly cares for you. Our anxieties are stoked when we don't trust that the Lord cares for us. Do you believe that he cares for you?

Casting your cares on God is an expression of moment-by-moment dependence on him, which is a fruit of humility. Why wait? Humble yourself before him right now and bring your anxieties to him.

Reflect: How might your anxiety show you your need for more grace?

Reflect: How would you describe your prayer life? What steps do you need to take to humble yourself?

Act: Prayerlessness is an indicator of pride and self-sufficiency. If this defines you, repent of it right now and ask the Lord for help.

DAY 22

Sober Up!

Be sober-minded; be watchful. Your adversary the devil prowls around like a roaring lion, seeking someone to devour. (1 Peter 5:8)

WEEDS OF ANXIETY flourish in the garden of pride, and the garden of pride is the devil's playground. That's the connection that Peter makes here. We saw yesterday that God "opposes the proud" (1 Peter 5:5) and commands us to "humble [ourselves]" (v. 6). Now Peter warns us to watch out for our adversary. Why? As it did for Lucifer (see Isa. 14:13–14), pride sets us up for a fall. Cultivating humility by casting our anxieties on God, however, defends us against the enemy of our souls (see 1 Peter 5:7).

All this reminds us that humility is of central importance to the Christian life. In his devotional classic, Andrew Murray writes, "Do not look at pride as only an unbecoming temper, nor at humility as only a decent virtue. The one is death, and the other is life; the one is all hell, the other is all heaven."[1] Pride is the reverse of Christlikeness. Trust in self and its frequent companion, anxiety, oppose trust in God. Thus, following the humble path of Jesus requires honest self-assessment. This is what Peter means when he tells us to "be sober-minded."

Sober-minded self-assessment helps us to control our emotions and fears. As Paul wrote, no one is to "think of himself more highly than he ought to think, but to think with sober judgment, each according to the measure of faith that God has assigned" (Rom. 12:3). Basically, humility entails having an accurate view of yourself so that you can honestly evaluate yourself from a biblical standpoint. This helps you to fight anxiety, because you see that only God is strong and capable enough to be relied on.

The entreaty to "be sober-minded; be watchful" emphasizes

the urgent need for you to be vigilant in your spiritual warfare—particularly by being aware of the ways that your spiritual adversary takes advantage of your particular bents or weaknesses. Don't be surprised that Satan wants you to live an anxiety-prone life. Three descriptors in today's verse reveal the insidiousness of his work.

Satan accuses. The devil "accuses [our brothers] day and night before our God" (Rev. 12:10). Our consciences' accusations are helpful (see Rom. 2:14–15), but Satan's are always destructive.

Satan slanders. He is "the devil" (*diabolos*). He is diabolical in his deception. As he did when he was with Eve, the devil's chief way to slander God is to whisper doubts about God's goodness and integrity (see Gen. 3:3–6).

Satan consumes. The devil "prowls around like a roaring lion." He is always hungry to "devour" believers. Like a lion that catches its prey off guard by moving slowly with its body close to the ground, Satan is always stalking.

Satan is also the father of lies (see John 8:44). It should be no surprise, then, that our pride and his deception often combine to create turmoil inside us.

Humility is not only our hearts' proper posture before the Lord; it is also a means by which we shield ourselves against attacks on our minds and souls. But often, we still fail—in our pride we give in to fear and temptation. What great comfort there is, then, in knowing that even when we sin with our emotions, we may turn again to our "advocate with the Father, Jesus Christ the righteous" (1 John 2:1).

Reflect: Self-trust and pride lead to a more anxious life.

Reflect: How do you see pride mixing with your anxiety? Are any other emotions particular points of vulnerability for you?

Act: Write a prayer. Confess your pride to the Lord and plead for him to give you an accurate self-assessment.

DAY 23

Entrust Yourself to God at Night

But you, O Lord, are a shield about me, my glory, and the lifter of my head. I cried aloud to the Lord, and he answered me from his holy hill. I lay down and slept; I woke again, for the Lord sustained me. (Ps. 3:3–5)

LOSS OF SLEEP is a common result of anxiety. We toss and turn, upset by what happened today and worried about what tomorrow might bring. Overdue bills. Relational conflict. Results of a family member's CT scan. Whatever the cause of our upset, anxiety is a thief. But there's a way to arrest what robs you of a good night's rest.

King David penned today's psalm when his son Absalom was leading a coup to seize David's throne (see 2 Sam. 15). In the grip of fear, after having fled Jerusalem, somehow the man after God's own heart "lay down and slept." How is that possible? His prayer in this psalm answers that question. It reveals three unchangeable truths that can act as spiritual sleep aids when you, in confident faith, entrust yourself to the Lord's safekeeping.[1]

God surrounds you like a shield. Absalom's cunning deception and smooth speech turned David's peaceful reign into wartime terror. Dissenters mocked him and God's so-called protection of him. But he prayed, "You, O Lord, are a shield about me" (v. 3). When your circumstances become fertile ground for fear to flourish, you need to follow David's example. Make a decisive shift in your focus *from* the attacks and accusations of the wicked *to* rock-solid truths about God. Fight fear with a greater fear—the fear of God. He is the invisible shield surrounding you.

God sustains you by your sleep. David's childlike trust in God as his protector led him to earnest prayer: "I cried aloud to the Lord" (v. 4). And God answered. He provided sleep for the rehabilitation of David's weary mind and body. God will do this for you, too. If you follow David's example of earnestness in prayer, his testimony can become yours: "I lay down and slept; I woke up, for it is Yahweh who keeps supporting me" (v. 5).[2] In a footnote to verse 5, Motyer provides an alternate translation of that last phrase as "the Lord my pillow!"[3] David rested *in* God and rested *on* God. This sustained rest then led him to greater confidence: "I will not be afraid of many thousands of people who have set themselves against me all around" (v. 6).

God secures you with his salvation. David knew that no matter what his enemies might do to him, God would always get the final word. Ultimately it was the Lord who would "strike" down his enemies and "break the teeth of the wicked" (v. 7). Striking the cheek signifies rebuke, and breaking their teeth signifies God's rendering his enemies harmless in the end.[4] In God's hands, enemies of his children are toothless tigers who may cause a lot of pain and trouble but ultimately cannot harm the ones whom God protects. All this leads to David's triumphant conclusion in the last verse: "To Yahweh belongs salvation!" and "Upon your people your blessing!" (v. 8).[5]

Remember: God watches over those who belong to him. Though he may lead you through dark valleys and deep waters, the Lord is always with you. Do not be afraid. Look to him. Say to yourself, "Go back to bed, my soul. Lie down and sleep. For the Lord is on my side."

Reflect: Anxiety robs you of sleep, but the fear of the Lord grants you rest.

Reflect: Do you trust that the Lord is on your side—protecting, sustaining, and rescuing you?

Act: Read Luke 12:4–7. Journal what it means to fear God more than anything else. What assurance does Jesus give?

DAY 24

Remember the Promises of God

"Fear not, for I have redeemed you; I have called you by name, you are mine. When you pass through the waters, I will be with you; and through the rivers, they shall not overwhelm you; when you walk through fire you shall not be burned, and the flame shall not consume you." (Isa. 43:1–2)

THE PROMISES OF God are like concrete pylons driven deep into the ocean floor. When waves of anxiety push us around or threaten to sink us, we may tie the rope of our faith to the immovable character of God, which his promises reveal. "Fear not," God says, and then he makes a promise.

The prophet Isaiah was given a tough assignment—to declare the displeasure that God felt toward his chosen people and to predict the judgment that they would receive. But, as it so often happens with God, mingled with this painful news are comforting promises of hope and restoration. Though these promises were made to Abraham's physical seed, they can also be applied to his spiritual seed—the "sons of Abraham" (Gal. 3:7)—that is, every Christian. You can fasten the rope of your faith to God's assurances.

God cares for you because he created you, redeemed you, and made you his own (see Isa. 43:1). You are precious to God because he redeemed you and adopted you into his family (see Gal. 4:4–5). He calls you by his name and has even given you a new name (see Rev. 2:17). He says, "You are mine."

God will be with you in your trials (see Isa. 43:2). He assured his chosen people that "when you pass through the waters, I will be with you." And today he assures you that "I will never leave you nor forsake you" (Heb. 13:5). Even if you walk through dark valleys, God is with you (see Ps. 23:4). He says, "You are not alone."

Your trials will not overtake you (see Isa. 43:2). God assured his people that he would be with them through rivers and fire. His presence would keep them from being overwhelmed, burned, or consumed. Though your faith is "tested by fire," you are being "guarded through faith" (see 1 Peter 1:5–7). In times of testing, you may be confident that God will "provide the way of escape, that you may be able to endure it" (1 Cor. 10:13). He says, "You are safe."

God's promises have the power to tame your emotions when you bank on them. Your anxieties scream, "God has forgotten you! You are alone! You are in danger!" They work overtime to distract you from what is true. But God assures you, "You are mine. You are not alone. You are safe." Do you trust in these promises? Will you anchor yourself to them? When your spiritual storehouse is well-stocked with promises like these, it will be more difficult for your heart to be overtaken by fear, and you will be more like the righteous man who "is not afraid of bad news," because your heart will be "firm, trusting in the LORD" (Ps. 112:7).

Reflect: In Isaiah 41, the Lord reassures his people that, though judgment is coming, they will not be cast off. His enduring presence is guaranteed: "Fear not, for I am with you; be not dismayed, for I am your God; I will strengthen you, I will help you, I will uphold you with my righteous right hand" (v. 10). How does this comfort you?

Act: Hook your life into a few more of God's promises: Psalm 18:30; 94:18–19; Hebrews 13:6. Memorize these promises, and let them be your anchors when you are afraid.

Act: Write your own prayer that communicates trust in God and his promises.

DAY 25

Cripple the Power of Fear with Faith

The LORD is my light and my salvation; whom shall I fear? The LORD is the stronghold of my life; of whom shall I be afraid? . . . One thing have I asked of the LORD, that will I seek after: that I may dwell in the house of the LORD all the days of my life, to gaze upon the beauty of the LORD and to inquire in his temple. (Ps. 27:1, 4)

ESCALATING ANXIETY SOMETIMES makes it seem impossible for us to respond in a righteous way. Pastor and author Brian Borgman explains, "Worry is a crippling emotion that paralyzes us. It bogs us down emotionally, making us virtually useless for anything else. In addition, it leads to other sins. 'Fret not yourself; it tends only to evil' (Ps. 37:8b). . . . Fear leads to lying, forgetting God, not trusting God, and not fearing God."[1] We don't always recognize this tendency and, if we do, don't always admit it. But anxiety *can* lead to other sins, as we saw in part 1 of this devotional.

That's why there is much to learn from Psalm 27. Conflict induces some of the highest levels of anxiety you will ever experience. As King David's enemies increased, so did his anxiety. Three times in the opening verses of this psalm he confesses to being afraid (see vv. 1–3). At least six times in the whole of the psalm he identifies the basis of his fear: evildoers, adversaries, armies at war, enemies, and false witnesses (see vv. 2, 3, 6, 12). Yet rather than responding with sin, David responds in a righteous manner, with a heart that is strengthened by God-centered faith. He turns to his only help and cries out to God (see v. 7). He fights fear with confidence in God as his defender.

How did he do this? What can we learn from his example?

Faith cripples the power of fear by reminding us of the right-now presence of the Lord (v. 1). David reminds himself that "the LORD *is* my light and my salvation" and that "the LORD *is* the stronghold of my life." In fear's grip, biblical faith doesn't look only to promises of *future* deliverance but to assurances of *present* protection. While being persecuted by enemies, David says, "God is here with me. In him I will put my trust. He is my protection."

Faith cripples the power of our fear when our focus and affection become singular in the Lord (v. 4). David deliberately turns the eyes of his heart away from real-life fears and toward his one, undying passion—to live in the real-time presence of the Lord. David seeks, "all the days of my life, to gaze upon the beauty of the LORD." As it was with David, so it can be with us. Gazing on the beauty of the Lord will rightly align our affections, enliven our faith, and alleviate our fears. Do you have that same singular longing—to seek after the Lord? Or does anxiety distract you from the Lord?

Faith is powerful, isn't it? It helps us to fight our fears as we find our confidence in the Lord.

Reflect: Do you, like David, have confidence that God is on your side?

Reflect: In what ways do you experience the crippling effects of fear? Do you see any tendencies in yourself to allow anxiety to lead you to sin in other ways? If so, are you ever tempted to excuse this?

Act: The second half of Psalm 27 (vv. 8–14) is an anxious prayer that expresses David's hope to see his longings of verses 1–7 come to final fruition as he sees "the goodness of the LORD in the land of the living" (v. 13). Can you pray this prayer and make it your own?

DAY 26

Trust in the Lord with All Your Heart

Trust in the LORD with all your heart, and do not lean on your own understanding. (Prov. 3:5)

TRUSTING GOD IS something that Christians talk about a lot, and yet we tend to view it as optional. There are times when we trust God and times when we don't, and we think that this is okay. But distrust is more serious than that; it positions us to trust in other things (see Ps. 20:7)—none of which deserve our trust. Distrust in God also makes us much more anxious. Like a ship in a storm without an anchor, we have a hard time weathering treacherous circumstances, because we're not centering our lives on Christ.

A better understanding of trust will help us here. Proverbs 3:5 points us to a robust biblical trust that helps us to fight our fears.

Trust is external ("in the LORD"). By calling it external, I mean that the foundation of trust is not inside us. Biblical trust is based on something—Someone—outside ourselves. Trusting God is not psyching ourselves up to believe the impossible. It involves resting on God's character. The only proper object of trust is God himself. Jeremiah explains, "Blessed is the man who trusts in the LORD" (Jer. 17:7). In contrast, there are innumerable objects of faith that are unworthy. These include, for example, man's strength (see Ps. 33:16–17), government leaders (see Ps. 146:3), wisdom and riches (see Jer. 9:23), and our own hearts (see Prov. 28:26). Who or what are you trusting in?

Trust is entire ("with *all* your heart"). According to Scripture, the *heart* includes the mind, emotions, and will. For that reason, biblical faith is the entrusting of our total being to God in submission to his Word. "You shall love the LORD your God with all your heart and with all your soul and with all your might" (Deut. 6:5). God promises blessing to those whose hearts' desire is to love him: "Blessed are those who keep his testimonies, who seek him with their whole heart" (Ps. 119:2). Have you given your whole life to the Lord?

Trust is exclusive ("do not lean on your own understanding"). It's natural for us to depend on our own reasoning and then act on it. However, great danger accompanies the trusting of self, as Hosea warns: "You have plowed wickedness, you have reaped injustice, you have eaten the fruit of lies. Because you have trusted in your way, in your numerous warriors" (Hos. 10:13 NASB). In God alone should we trust. Are you trusting in yourself or in the Lord?

Your fears can keep you from trusting God. "God won't care for me." "I'll never be married." "I won't survive the cancer." "I won't make enough to provide or to get us out of debt." Your worries roll around in your heart and mind, telling you to trust in yourself and in "your own understanding," because God must not be enough.

But the Lord himself beckons you: "Trust in me. Let me be your refuge and strength—your very present help in times of trouble" (see Ps. 46:1). Rather than letting your fears run rampant, commit to trusting the Lord today with your whole life.

Reflect: What fears keep you from trusting God? When you are anxious, what does your heart desire more than God?

Reflect: In what ways do you tend to lean on your own understanding?

Act: Find a mature Christian and ask him or her, "How have you grown in your trust of the Lord?"

DAY 27

Acknowledge the Lord in All Your Ways

In all your ways acknowledge him, and he will
make straight your paths. (Prov. 3:6)

WORRYING ABOUT THE future is the opposite of trusting in the Lord. When we worry about tomorrow, we are more likely to lean on our own understanding—to attempt to control (at least in our minds) what is outside our control. When Jesus commands us, "Do not be anxious," one reason he gives for this is that worry brings the potential problems of tomorrow into today. But "sufficient for the day is its own trouble" (Matt. 6:34). Instead we should plan and live as wisely as Scripture directs, all the while trusting the Lord to lead us according to his kind intentions.

We express this trust when we daily acknowledge the Lord in all our ways. "Ways" refers to a journey. The Christian life is a faith journey—a daily walk that eventually adds up to months, years, and decades. The New Living Translation of this verse reads, "Seek his will in all you do, and he will show you which path to take." The reward of our daily dependence on the Lord is that we will be able to look back and see how—though the hills and turns may have appeared to be too difficult—he was faithfully making our paths straight.

As we seek God's will, we learn to walk by faith and not sight (see 2 Cor. 5:7). As God leads us and his grace brings us around twists in the road, we see his beauty, wisdom, and goodness in fresh ways. This is how it happened for Job. After major turns of unspeakable suffering, Job saw God in a new light and testified, "I had heard of you by the hearing of the ear, but now my eye sees you" (Job 42:5). Before Job's time of severe testing, he had heard *about* God. But now, after God rebuked him, he *saw* God—he learned firsthand what his faithful, living Redeemer was really like (see Job 19:25–27). We need to remember that, even though from our perspective the journey appears to turn here and there and even reverse at times, God's viewpoint is bigger. Despite every turn, he points our path straight toward the fulfillment of his will.

One essential way for us to seek God's guidance is to plead with him in prayer: "Lead me, O LORD, in your righteousness because of my enemies; make your way straight before me" (Ps 5:8); "Lead me in your truth and teach me, for you are the God of my salvation; for you I wait all the day long" (Ps 25:5); "Teach me your way, O LORD, and lead me on a level path because of my enemies" (Ps 27:11); "Teach me to do your will, for you are my God! Let your good Spirit lead me on level ground!" (Ps 143:10). When you lean into the Lord through prayer and you trust him to answer, you can rest in his assurances. He will do the following:

- guide you into pleasant paths (see Ps. 23:1–2).
- guide your decision making (see Ps. 25:8–9).
- guide you through the end of your life (see Ps. 48:14).
- guide you by wise counsel (see Ps. 73:24).
- guide you into an understanding of truth (see Ps. 143:10; John 16:13).

Don't worry about the future. Acknowledge God in all your ways, and he will "make straight your paths."

Reflect: How do you need to grow in your acknowledging of the Lord in all your ways?

Act: Read Psalm 37:3–5. Journal the actions that you need to take and the promises that God will fulfill.

DAY 28

Relax in God

"Be still, and know that I am God. I will be exalted among the nations, I will be exalted in the earth!" The LORD of hosts is with us; the God of Jacob is our fortress. (Ps. 46:10–11)

REPLACING ANXIETY WITH peace involves a choice. We must *stop* being anxious. We must *quiet ourselves.* We must *deliberately shift* the focal point of our attention. Inner peace doesn't simply happen to us while we are being passive. Our will must be actively engaged. God makes this clear when he says, "Be still, and know that I am God."

"Be still" may also be translated "Cease striving" (NASB). The Hebrew word that is translated "cease" means to sink or relax. And "striving" is a term that typically refers to warfare. God's admonition may be stated this way: "Be at peace. Relax. I am God. You are not. I am the conqueror. I am Lord of all the earth. And I am all of this . . . for your personal safety." This warrior imagery stirred Martin Luther to write the hymn "A Mighty Fortress Is Our God." God is our fortress; he is a military stronghold—an impenetrable building where we can run to hide. He is our bulwark; he is a stockade—a wall of defense against earthly and spiritual enemies.

The theme of finding shelter in God permeates Psalm 46. Truly he is "our refuge and strength, a very present help in trouble" (v. 1). "Therefore [because verse 1 is true] we will not fear" (v. 2). But the psalmist also reveals how we can plug into a real-time sense of God's safekeeping power. He counsels us to "come, behold the works of the LORD" (v. 8). When we feel that our lives are in an upheaval, we can experience God's peace by remembering his powerful deeds.

The way for us to "be still," God says, is by knowing and

trusting him. It's by truly believing that he is who he says he is. He is God. He is sovereign. He is in control. We are not. Therefore, we can rest. We can relax in our hearts, souls, minds, and bodies. The more we behold the works of the Lord (and consciously meditate on them), the more confident we become. God is saying to us, "Stop worrying! I will have the victory. Stop acting as if this is your battle. Relax. Rest in me. Not only am I the God of the universe, but I am your God. I will be your peace." The psalm ends by repeating a key truth: "The LORD of hosts is with us; the God of Jacob is our fortress." God's presence is real. He is not far away. He is with us in all our trials, griefs, life changes, and anxieties. He is very near to us.

Anxiety hinders our faith and clouds our focus. It disables us. It doesn't want us to see the good works of the Lord. But we can put an end to worry by relaxing in God—by replacing our fears about tomorrow with confidence in the One who is in control today. We must remember the great works that God has done—not only in the earth but in our own lives. Chiefly, let us remember his *greatest* accomplishment—the redemption of our souls through the work of his Son!

Reflect: Resting in God involves pondering the many ways he has providentially cared for us, satisfied our needs, and demonstrated his power, love, and grace. What are some of the ways you have seen God's faithfulness at work over the course of your life?

Act: Begin a "works of God" section in your journal. List as many of these works as you can think of, and leave a few extra pages so that you can return to add more.

Act: If you are struggling to see the ways that God cares for you, find a mature Christian friend and ask him or her, "How do you see the grace of God in my life?"

DAY 29

Always Remember and Never Forget

Bless the LORD, O my soul, and forget not all his benefits. (Ps. 103:2)

IN TODAY'S PSALM, David gives us an example of how to speak to our own souls (see v. 1) and "forget not all [the Lord's] benefits" (v. 2). He models the way that doctrinally rich, God-centered songs speak truth to our souls by reminding us of God's love. As we consciously praise God, we shift our mind's eye from anxious cares to divine blessings that we must always remember and never forget. Consider some of the benefits this psalm mentions that come to you only from the Lord.

- God forgives all your iniquities (see v. 3).
- God will heal all your diseases (see v. 3)—in either this life or the life to come (see 1 Cor. 15:53).
- God redeems your life (not only your soul) from the pit of destruction and hopelessness (see v. 4).
- God crowns you with his steadfast love, is kind to you, and shows mercy to you (see v. 4).
- God fills you with good things; he will satisfy your soul (see v. 5).
- God renews your strength, causing you to soar like the eagle (see v. 5).
- God acts in righteousness and justice toward the oppressed (see v. 6).
- God is merciful and gracious to you (see v. 8).
- God is slow to anger when you sin (see v. 8).
- God abounds in lovingkindness toward you (see v. 8). He doesn't just sprinkle it; he pours it out.
- God will not hold on to his anger against you (see v. 9).

Remember that it has already been satisfied (propitiated) in Jesus (see Rom. 3:25).

- God has not treated you as your sins deserve (see v. 10).
- God's lovingkindness is great toward those who fear him (see vv. 11, 17).
- God has removed your transgressions, and their punishments, far away from you (see v. 12).
- God knows you and has compassion on your weakened frame (see vv. 13–14).
- God's lovingkindness is eternal (see v. 17).
- God's righteousness is to children's children (see v. 17). He will be faithful to his promises.
- God's sovereign rule remains over all—including every detail of your life (see v. 19).

Both before and after listing these benefits of knowing God, the psalmist tells himself to "Bless the LORD, O my soul!" These bookends of praise remind us of the importance of speaking biblical truth to ourselves in order to feed our faith.

How is deliberate praise an act of faith and a remedy for anxiety at the same time? It shifts our focus from the object of our worries (such as sickness, job stress, financial troubles, or a fight last night with our spouse) to the One who is sovereign over all things. Your worries lure you away from God, while praise shifts "all that is within" you (v. 1) to the Lord.

Reflect: We are much more prone to ask things of God than to praise him. In what ways do you need to remind your soul of God's steadfast love and mercy? What God-centered benefits has the Lord granted to you?

Act: Follow today's example of how to mine riches out of a passage of Scripture by reading Psalm 121 and listing the ways in which God is your helper.

DAY 30

Keep Yourself in God's Love

But you, beloved, building yourselves up in your most holy faith and praying in the Holy Spirit, keep yourselves in the love of God, waiting for the mercy of our Lord Jesus Christ that leads to eternal life. (Jude 20–21)

MEDITATING ON THE love of our triune God is a remedy for anxiety. We rest in the *Father's* steadfast love: "See what kind of love the Father has given to us, that we should be called children of God" (1 John 3:1). We also remember the *Son's* love for us, which was dramatically displayed in his voluntary death in our place (see John 10:18). And we appreciate the ministry of the *Holy Spirit*, who reassures us of God's love by testifying to our spirits that we are children of God (see Rom. 8:16).

In light of such a display of divine grace, we find a curious phrase: "Keep yourselves in the love of God" (Jude 21). Jude commands us to remain within the circle of God's love. This does not mean that your eternal salvation is dependent on your keeping yourself saved. Jude makes this clear in his greeting: "To those who are called, beloved in God the Father and kept for Jesus Christ" (Jude 1). Believers in Jesus are already being kept *for* him *by* God. Other Scriptures testify to this security.[1] Instead, this phrase means maintaining God-centered focus while prayerfully obeying the Word and waiting for Jesus to return. Jude teaches us that his main command to "keep yourselves in the love of God" is carried out through three disciplines.

Building yourself up "in your most holy faith" means growing in your understanding and application of sound doctrine. It means to be "rooted and built up in him and established in the faith" (see Col. 2:7) so that you may mature in Christ (see Eph. 4:13–14). Christian maturity is like a building's solid foundation.

Worries may come and go, but they won't overrun us, because we're grounded in Christ.

Praying in the Holy Spirit means praying according to the Word. As you submit your heart and life to the authority of the Scriptures, the Spirit fills (controls) you (see Eph. 5:17–18). One fruit of his control is a life that is soaked in prayer. Persevering in prayer is essential to arming yourself against the devil (see Eph. 6:18) and against all the worries that plague you. Through all this, you can confidently rest in the Spirit to pray for you (see Rom. 8:26–27). A worry-filled life can be prayerless. But a prayerful life takes every concern to the Lord out of confidence in his care (see 1 Peter 5:7).

Waiting for the Lord's return is not passive; it requires living with constant expectancy. No man knows when Jesus will come again (see Mark 13:32). Rather than setting our eyes on the temporal concerns of this life, and thereby growing our anxiety, we set our focus on the end, when Christ will return. This expectancy fuels holiness and hope in the believer (see Luke 12:40; Phil. 3:20; 1 John 2:28). It's a countermeasure to our worries.

We keep ourselves in the love of God through these disciplines. However, as Jude helpfully concludes, God ultimately preserves our faith. "[He] is able to keep you from stumbling and to present you blameless before the presence of his glory with great joy" (Jude 24).

Reflect: Read Jude 24–25. How do the closing verses of Jude's letter bring you hope?

Act: In what ways do you need to grow in these three disciplines? If you feel weak in these areas, go to a wise Christian and ask him or her to teach and mentor you in your faith.

DAY 31

Call Your Security Guard

"In my distress I called upon the LORD*; to my God I called. From his temple he heard my voice, and my cry came to his ears." (2 Sam. 22:7)*

PRESSURE PRODUCES PRAYER. Though prayer should be a consistent spiritual discipline in our lives at all times, nothing evokes it quite as much as trouble or distress. In the song of David that is recorded in 2 Samuel 22, we immediately perceive his distress, but we also notice his determination to call on the Lord.

In this thanksgiving psalm, King David praises the Lord for being his rock, fortress, and deliverer—one who, at numerous times, saved him from his enemies (see vv. 2–4). David's allusion to trouble is comprehensive; it's not limited to just one high-stress situation. Repeatedly throughout the song, David lifts up the Lord as his personal warrior.

Nestled within his extolling words is an insight into David's heart that is vital to an understanding of how his faith functionally conquered his fear. In his distress (a state of being in serious trouble, which includes mental strain and stress), David "called upon the LORD" as his "stronghold"—his personal security guard. Given the number of times that he found himself in agonizing circumstances throughout his life, calling on the Lord became a habit for David. It was how he fought back the crippling power of fear. And how did God respond to David's call? "From his temple he heard my voice, and my cry came to his ears" (v. 7). The Hebrew word for *heard* portrays God as attentively listening to the cries of David's heart. Truly, his "cry came to [God's] ears." Calling on the Lord is not only a remedy for anxiety but is also essential to walking in God's will (see 1 Thess. 5:17–18). When you are afraid, do you, like David, call upon the Lord?

It brings God pleasure to listen attentively to the cries of his children!

Yet something even more comforting is true. We may also rest assured that Jesus understands our need, because he has walked the same road, and that he prays for us. Psalm 18 (a variation of 2 Samuel 22 for public worship) is rich with foreshadowing of the Messiah. As such, it is quoted in the New Testament as applying to Jesus (see Rom. 15:9; Heb. 2:13). How fitting it is, then, that Jesus is every believer's faithful High Priest who "is able to save to the uttermost those who draw near to God through him, since he always lives to make intercession for them" (Heb. 7:25). It was this assurance that led minister Robert Murray M'Cheyne to conclude, "If I could hear Christ praying for me in the next room, I would not fear a million enemies. Yet distance makes no difference. He is praying for me."[1] In Christ, we have a personal security guard who will "hide [us] in his shelter in the day of trouble; he will conceal [us] under the cover of his tent" (Ps. 27:5).

Reflect: How confident are you that God hears you when you cry out to him?

Reflect: Any battle plan for anxiety that does not include constant prayer is inherently powerless against the fears that will repeatedly arise. What words would you currently use to describe your prayer life? What changes should you make to it?

Act: Read through Psalm 18 with your "Jesus glasses" on. Look for examples of how the sufferings of Jesus and his trust-filled response to God were foreshadowed by the words and experiences of King David.

Act: Pray through David's song and make it your own.

CONCLUSION

"Return, O My Soul, to Your Rest"

WE BEGAN OUR 31-day journey by thinking about the emotional honesty of Scripture. Anxiety and its cousins (fear, panic, and worry) are common in our human experience. There is no benefit to minimizing or denying this. They hurt your life.

We then walked down various roads of biblical insight, help, and counsel. Through it all, we've learned that fighting anxiety with the sufficiency of God's grace requires the discipline of biblical meditation. God's Word is powerful. You need to consistently turn back to it, and meditate on it, as you do battle with your worries.

Biblical meditation involves talking to ourselves—doing what the psalmist does in Psalm 116:7: "Return, O my soul, to your rest; for the LORD has dealt bountifully with you." Your faith grows as you become more secure in God's love by speaking scriptural truth to your anxious soul. On what basis does the psalmist remind his soul to rest? He remembers the Lord's kindness. Just as the psalmist did, remind yourself of how gracious the Lord has been—and continues to be—in his relationship with you.

But what does "returning to rest" look like? How do we exercise spiritual remembrance, practically speaking? As we fight worries, how do we recall God's goodness to us? Let me leave you with four admonitions.

Remember the Certainty of God's Promises

God's promises are rock-solid truths that can always be trusted, because they reflect his reliable character and his sovereignty. Charles Spurgeon once said, "To enjoy peace, our unbelieving thoughts must be stilled, and we must learn that the Lord reigns."[1] In Christ we are blessed beyond measure, "For all the promises of God find their Yes in him" (2 Cor. 1:20). Reflect on the faithfulness of God, and cultivate a heart of gratitude for all that belongs to you in Jesus Christ (see Eph. 2:6–7).

Remember the Grace of Salvation

The peace *of* God flows from our being at peace *with* God. Therefore, reflect on the amazing grace of God that was activated by his redemptive love for you (see John 3:16–18). Never take for granted the gift of his Son, who died in your place, endured God's wrath against your sin, and was raised from the dead in order to give you new life. Jesus did all of this to publicly demonstrate that free admission to God's presence now belongs to those who trust Christ (see Rom. 4:25; 1 Peter 3:18; 1 John 4:10). It is through Jesus alone that you "have also obtained access by faith into this grace in which we stand, and we rejoice in hope of the glory of God" (Rom. 5:2).

Remember the Care of Your Heavenly Father

When anxious cares distract your soul from holding on to God as your highest devotion, don't ever forget that the heavenly Father knows all your needs and loves you more than you realize (Matt. 6:25–34). When these same distractions tug down your hope and squelch your joy, remember him who gave you his greatest treasure: "He who did not spare his own Son but gave him up for us all, how will he not also with him graciously give us all things? (Rom. 8:32).

Remember Your Dependency on Prayer

Cast your anxieties on the Lord (see 1 Peter 5:7) and let the peace of God rule your heart (see Phil. 4:6–7). Kill the pride of independence by cultivating constancy in your prayer life (see 1 Thess. 5:17). Call on the Lord whenever you are in distress (see Ps. 18). Ask God to make turning to him in prayer your normal response to worry.

The battle against anxiety requires ongoing discipline: renewing your mind with biblical truth, shifting your heart's affections to God, and refreshing your soul with the wellspring of grace. You can't be passive in your fight against anxiety. It's far too easy for worries to overtake your life. As you feed your soul with Scripture, lean into God as your trustworthy caregiver, and cultivate a heart of thanksgiving, you will progressively notice your anxiety fading in comparison to the peace that is found in Jesus.

Where Do You Go from Here?

We're almost finished. Battling anxiety and worries is a lifetime of work. Now that the devotional is done, what do you do?

Reread This Devotional

Anxiety is like an infestation of pesky termites that don't go away. You find victory, grow in your trust in the Lord, and put to death many of your worries—but months later, you find them creeping back in. If that happens, come back to this devotional again and reread it to strengthen you in times of worry.

Take Ownership of Scripture

We have studied thirty-one texts and seen their relevance to our anxiety. If there are a few Scriptures that the Holy Spirit has especially used to help you, take ownership of these texts. Memorize them. Meditate on them. Write them on a 3x5 card and pull them out whenever you are struggling. Pray through them. And share them with close friends. Make them an integral part of your fight with worry.

Join a Gospel-Preaching Church

If you are not attending a gospel-preaching church, then the most important thing you can do for your soul is to join one. The Christian life is never meant to be an individual venture. Our anxieties are best fought in the context of a loving, Christ-centered, gospel-rich community. Find a local church that is committed to proclaiming God's Word as truth, and then join it. Go every week so that your soul is fed with truth.

Don't Fight This Battle on Your Own

A number of the devotions asked you to reach out to a pastor or a mature Christian friend. "Whoever isolates himself seeks his own desire; he breaks out against all sound judgment" (Prov. 18:1). Isolating yourself leads you to focus only on your desires. As you join a gospel-preaching church, commit to getting to know other believers and to letting them get to know you. Take the risk of exposing your troubles to others and of giving them the opportunity to love you in return.

If Your Anxieties Are Crippling, Seek Help

When anxieties are ruining your life, that's a good time to find a Christ-centered counselor. Humility is required for taking this next step, and pride can get in the way. God opposes the proud and shows grace to the humble (see James 4:6).

Read the Resources Listed at the Back of the Book

If you want more to read, check out the mini-books and books that are listed in the Suggested Resources section. Why not include in your reading each year a solid booklet or book about fighting anxiety?

Take a Long-Term View of Your Worries

As a fellow struggler, I leave you with a final thought to ponder. Since we dwell in fallen bodies that walk about in a fallen world, our anxiety will never be completely eliminated . . . for now. But a day is coming when we will be completely set free from all weakness and sin. Picture this: in glory, we will dwell with the Lord and worship him in unhindered fellowship for all eternity.

> And I heard a loud voice from the throne saying, "Behold, the dwelling place of God is with man. He will dwell with them, and they will be his people, and God himself will be with them as their God. He will wipe away every tear from their eyes, and death shall be no more, neither shall there be mourning, nor crying, nor pain anymore, for the former things have passed away." (Rev. 21:3–4)

The Lord will take away our tears. There will be no sin or suffering anymore, so there will be no more death, mourning, crying, or pain. So also, there will be no anxiety. What a marvelous thought—no more struggle! The only thing that will matter is our worship of the Lord.

As we wait for that glorious day, we must keep saying to ourselves, "Return, O my soul, to your rest; for the LORD has dealt bountifully with you." Let's keep reminding ourselves of the goodness of the Lord as we fight our anxieties.

Acknowledgments

I'm thankful for my wife, Karen, who has stood by me in steadfast faithfulness and grace for over three decades of marriage and for almost the same length of time in Christian ministry. Her unfailing love for God, first, and for then me, during times of both joy and pain, furnishes me with strength and encouragement. She is truly a helper who was custom designed by God for me. In heaven, her reward will be great, for "her works praise her in the gates" (Prov. 31:31).

I'm thankful also for my children and their spouses, whose steady honor, friendship, and progress in Christ humble me. For my friends who have shown me what Christian love looks like—Solomon did not exaggerate your value. Truly "there is a friend who sticks closer than a brother" (Prov. 18:24). And for the sanctifying influence of those same friends. Again, Solomon did not overestimate your worth. "Faithful are the wounds of a friend; profuse are the kisses of an enemy" (Prov. 27:6).

For the congregation of Cornerstone Community Church, whose love for Christ, the Word, and one another has created an atmosphere of joy and sanctifying grace. For my fellow elders, who exemplify Christlike love, godly character, loyalty to Scripture, and the fruit of the Spirit. My family knows it is an honor to be part of a church family that has "been taught by God to love one another" (1 Thess. 4:9).

Most of all, I'm thankful for the remarkable providence of the Lord, whose divine orchestration of my life is mind-boggling. My Savior's combination of sovereignty, wisdom, and goodness has never failed me. The psalmist speaks for me:

> The Lord is my chosen portion and my cup;
>   you hold my lot.
> The lines have fallen for me in pleasant places;
>   indeed, I have a beautiful inheritance. (Ps. 16:5–6)

Notes

Tips for Reading This Devotional

1. See Jonathan Leeman, *Reverberation: How God's Word Brings Light, Freedom, and Action to His People* (Chicago: Moody, 2011), 19.

Introduction: When Panic Attacks

1. See "Broken Heart Syndrome," Mayo Clinic, accessed March 1, 2018, http://www.mayoclinic.org/diseases-conditions/broken-heart-syndrome/symptoms-causes/syc-20354617.
2. To see more about how Paul's mental suffering was a consequence of his physical suffering, read the context of this verse in 2 Cor. 1:8–11; 11:16–33.
3. When David says in verse 13 that God uniquely forms our "inward parts," the Hebrew word used here refers to our emotional nature.

A Brief Word on Medication

1. Two books written by Christian physicians that provide helpful insight in this regard are Charles D. Hodges, *Good Mood, Bad Mood: Help and Hope for Depression and Bipolar Disorder* (Wapwallopen, PA: Shepherd Press, 2013), and Michael R. Emlet, *Descriptions and Prescriptions: A Biblical Perspective on Psychiatric Diagnoses and Medications* (Greensboro, NC: New Growth Press, 2017).
2. Quoted in Laura Hendrickson, "The Complex Mind/Body Connection," in *Christ-Centered Biblical Counseling: Changing Lives with God's Changeless Truth*, ed. James MacDonald, Bob Kellemen, and Steve Viars (Eugene, OR: Harvest House Publishers, 2013), 421. You can read Bob's book-length testimony in Robert B. Somerville, *If I'm a Christian, Why Am I Depressed? Finding Meaning and Hope in the Dark Valley; One Man's Journey* (Maitland, FL: Xulon Press, 2014).

Day 5: Disordered Worship

1. Joseph S. Carroll, *How to Worship Jesus Christ: Experiencing His Manifest Presence Daily* (Greenville, SC: Great Commission, 1984), 29.

Day 6: Discontent and Coveting

1. Walter A. Elwell, ed., *Baker Encyclopedia of the Bible*, vol. 1, A–I (Grand Rapids: Baker Book House, 1988), 539.

Day 8: Perfectionism May Cause Anxiety

1. Both a striving for excellence and a diligent work ethic are good in their proper place. It's the performance-driven motivation that's an issue here.

Day 14: Your Heavenly Father Knows

1. Philip De Courcy, *HELP! I'm Anxious* (Wapwallopen, PA: Shepherd Press, 2018), 18.

Day 15: Choose to Rejoice

1. Selena Rezvani, "Why Complaining Is Killing Your Reputation at Work," *Forbes*, July 11, 2014, https://www.forbes.com/sites/work-in-progress/2014/07/11/why-complaining-is-killing-your-reputation-at-work/#1aca7a324bb9.
2. See Walter A. Elwell, ed., *Baker Encyclopedia of the Bible*, vol. 2, J–Z (Grand Rapids, MI: Baker Book House, 1988), 1224.

Day 16: Worry about Nothing; Pray about Everything

1. D. Martyn Lloyd-Jones, *Spiritual Depression: Its Causes and Its Cure* (Grand Rapids: Wm. B. Eerdmans Publishing Company, 1965), 82.

Day 17: Find Peace through Prayer

1. Jesus is the vine, and we are the branches (see John 15:5).

Day 20: Kill Worry with Daggers of Truth

1. Paul Tautges, *Counseling One Another: A Theology of Interpersonal Discipleship* (Wapwallopen, PA: Shepherd Press, 2016), 77.

Day 22: Sober Up!

1. Andrew Murray, *Humility* (repr., New Kensington, PA: Whitaker House, 1982), 97–98.

Day 23: Entrust Yourself to God at Night

1. For this simple outline of Psalm 3, I am indebted to Dr. William Varner of The Master's University in Santa Clarita, California. See

William Varner, "Psalm Three 'Advice for Insomniacs,'" Facebook, September 24, 2016, https://www.facebook.com/william.varner .12/posts/10157391347140468.

2. Translation given in Alec Motyer, *Psalms by the Day: A New Devotional Translation* (Fearn, UK: Christian Focus, 2016), 16.
3. Motyer, 16n12.
4. See Motyer, 16.
5. Translation given in Motyer, 16.

Day 25: Cripple the Power of Fear with Faith

1. Brian S. Borgman, *Feelings and Faith: Cultivating Godly Emotions in the Christian Life* (Wheaton, IL: Crossway Books, 2009), 126.

Day 30: Keep Yourself in God's Love

1. We see that Christians are kept by the power of God for an eternal inheritance (see 1 Peter 1:3–5), are gifts from the Father to the Son (see John 10:29; 17:9, 24), can never be separated from God's love (see Rom. 8:31–39), and are permanently sealed by the Holy Spirit (see Eph. 1:13–14; 4:30). He is the down payment of their redemption—the security of more to come.

Day 31: Call Your Security Guard

1. Andrew Bonar, *Robert Murray M'Cheyne* (Edinburgh: Banner of Truth, 1960), 179.

Conclusion: "Return, O My Soul, to Your Rest"

1. Charles H. Spurgeon, *Morning and Evening: A New Edition of the Classic Devotional Based on The Holy Bible, English Standard Version*, rev. and updated Alistair Begg (Wheaton, IL: Crossway, 2003), available online at "Blameless!" Truth For Life, October 10, 2018, https://www.truthforlife.org/resources/daily-devotionals /10/10/0/.

Suggested Resources for the Fight

Booklets and Mini-Books

De Courcy, Philip. *HELP! I'm Anxious.* Wapwallopen, PA: Shepherd Press, 2018. [A very encouraging exposition and application of the portion of the Sermon on the Mount in which Jesus teaches on worry. It contains practical application projects that help worriers to apply God's promises. In addition to personal study, this resource is excellent for counseling and small groups.]

Jones, Robert D. *Why Worry? Getting to the Heart of Your Anxiety.* Phillipsburg, NJ: P&R Publishing, 2018. [Robert Jones, a pastor, biblical counselor, and seminary professor, explains and applies the words of Jesus on worry. He also shares encouraging stories from fellow worriers who found comfort in God's Word.]

Kellemen, Robert W. *Anxiety: Anatomy and Cure.* Phillipsburg, NJ: P&R Publishing, 2012. [Biblical counselor and pastor Bob Kellemen teaches us how to deal honestly with our emotions while calling us to a lifestyle of surrendering them daily to the mind of Christ.]

Newheiser, Jim. *HELP! I Need a Church.* Wapwallopen, PA: Shepherd Press, 2016. [Long-time pastor and counselor Jim Newheiser provides biblical and practical guidance on how to find a local church that will nurture your faith and help you to grow in your relationship with Christ.]

Powlison, David. *Worry: Pursuing a Better Path to peace.* Phillipsburg, NJ: P&R Publishing, 2004. [David Powlison, a biblical counselor and trainer, delves into the inner workings of worry and shows how Jesus is the only true source of peace.]

Books

Duguid, Barbara R. *Streams of Mercy: Prayers of Confession and Celebration.* Edited by Iain M. Duguid. Phillipsburg, NJ: P&R Publishing, 2018. [In the likeness of the Puritan classic *The Valley of Vision*, this fresh collection of scriptural calls to confession, prayers, and pardons will enrich your personal devotions.]

MacArthur, John. *FOUND: God's Peace; Experience True Freedom from Anxiety in Every Circumstance.* Colorado Springs: David C. Cook, 2015. [MacArthur shares principles to help you overcome anxiety and stresses the importance of replacing worry with prayer, right thinking, and application of God's Word.]

Tautges, Paul. *Pray About Everything: Cultivating God-Dependency.* Wapwallopen, PA: Shepherd Press, 2017. [A book that aims to call believers to a life of God-dependency, which we practice most readily by learning to pray biblically.]

Welch, Edward T. *Running Scared: Fear, Worry, and the God of Rest.* Greensboro, NC: New Growth Press, 2007. [Explores how fear takes root in all of our lives—and how our race for the good life finds us, all too often, "running scared." The author encourages us to discover how the Bible is filled with beautiful words of comfort and peace for fearful people.]

31-Day Devotionals for Life

A Series

Deepak Reju
Series Editor

Addictive Habits: Changing for Good, by David R. Dunham
After an Affair: Pursuing Restoration, by Michael Scott Gembola
Anger: Calming Your Heart, by Robert D. Jones
Anxiety: Knowing God's Peace, by Paul Tautges
Assurance: Resting in God's Salvation, by William P. Smith
Contentment: Seeing God's Goodness, by Megan Hill
Doubt: Trusting God's Promises, by Elyse Fitzpatrick
Fearing Others: Putting God First, by Zach Schlegel
Grief: Walking with Jesus, by Bob Kellemen
Money: Seeking God's Wisdom, by Jim Newheiser
Pornography: Fighting for Purity, by Deepak Reju

Was this book helpful to you?
Consider writing a review online.
The author appreciates your feedback!

Or write to P&R at editorial@prpbooks.com
with your comments. We'd love to hear from you.